It's alright now – God is in charge!

Patricia Margretta Cassidy

It's alright now – God is in charge!

Onwards and Upwards Publishers

Berkeley House,
11 Nightingale Crescent,
Leatherhead,
Surrey, KT24 6PD.
www.onwardsandupwards.org

First edition published in 2013.
Second edition published in 2013.

Printed in the UK

ISBN:	978-1-907509-93-3
Typeface:	Sabon LT
Graphic design:	Leah-Maarit

Dedication

In memory of my wonderful parents to whom I owe so much,
Ralph Wallace and Margretta Sheila Lee.

For my dear grandchildren – Jonathan, Luke, Charlotte, Katherine, William, Rebecca and Jessica – with real appreciation and thanks for your loving encouragement and support! And also, now, for Emily Rose, Samuel James and any subsequent precious great-grandchildren!

This book is to tell you of a remarkable era, now almost a time of history, with a firsthand account about some of your forebears and a little of how life was for your grandmother and great-grandparents around the Second World War and afterwards.

I also want to tell you all something that I have experienced of the amazing love of God and how real I have found Jesus Christ is as my Saviour, in every sense of that wonderful word! There have been remarkable answers to prayers all through my life, and I trust that my story will show this in a great many ways.

I know that He loves each of us far more than we can ever realise while on this earth and that we each need to search for this Truth for ourselves. God does not have grandchildren, or great-grandchildren, but He does have children to whom He longs to be Father in a deep and loving relationship. Every one of us can become a child of God, through Jesus who died in our place, so that we can be with Him forever. Whether we will accept this truth has to be our choice, and my prayer for you throughout your lives, each of my 'fave' grandchildren, is that you will make this choice and accept all that love, and so also come to know His reality and joy!

Endorsements

This beautifully written book has been hard to put down. I have read many autobiographies but this one stands out. Whilst a very personal story, the backdrop of World War II and the author's journey of faith bring so many insights on the journey of life that are relevant for us all today.

Many times the family was brought to the edge through separation and the uncertainties of war yet their faith continued to deepen and became the bedrock of their lives. The importance of having parents and grandparents to bring encouragement on the faith-journey of life is very clear; truly knowing Jesus alongside makes all the difference.

It is easy for today's young people to forget the impact of war, the challenge of getting to know one's father again when he returns home bearing the trauma of POW camp, the day to day wondering if he is alive – no electronic communication to bring reassurance!

I can't wait for the sequel that hopefully will be written, telling us of the author's beautiful, God-given ministry over subsequent decades. Reading this book will enrich your life, and I'm sure you will then want to pass it on to others.

Dr Gareth Tuckwell
Chairman Friend of Vellore UK
Former CEO, Burrswood Christian Hospital
Trustee, Macmillan Cancer Support

I count it a great privilege to know Patsy both as a friend and as the pastor of her church. But it was only recently that I learned what a remarkable life she has led. Her family have had to face a number of terrifying situations that drove them to their knees, and it was at those moments that Patsy experienced first-hand the power and faithfulness of God. I invite you to read this book in which she recounts the twists and turns of her international adventure. I'm sure that just like me, you will be fascinated by her extraordinary story.

Reverend James Packman
Rector of St Albans Church in the village of Frant

Acknowledgements

With acknowledgements and warmest thanks to my many friends for all their prayers and encouragement, and also to:

Both **Jenny Cooper** and **Brian Woodgate** for their patient help in editing; their advice, wisdom and time and, particularly, for encouraging me to have this book published;

To **Audrey Dicker** for her painstaking skill in proof-reading;

To **Jennifer Rees Larcombe** for enthusiastically writing the Foreword;

To **Dr Gareth Tuckwell** and the **Rev James Packman** for very kindly writing their endorsements;

To the team at **Onwards and Upwards** for making publishing this book interesting and enjoyable, and for being so helpful;

All these dear friends are much appreciated for their love and generosity in giving so much of their time.

Contents

It's alright now – God is in charge!

Foreword by Jennifer Rees Larcombe

I have known Patsy Cassidy for many years as we have worked together in ministry and counselling. She has a very beautiful spirit, and her book is as full of love and grace as she is herself! She has not only brought to life a valuable piece of history but also told a captivating story, very well indeed!

Patsy's father worked for the Hong Kong and Shanghai Bank so the book is packed with a wealth of period detail and local colour from Far East postings during the inter-war years. It also contains some fascinating contemporary reactions to news at home concerning the abdication crisis and the lead up to World War II. Patsy keeps us enthralled with everything from tiger 'adventures' and landslides in Malaya, a doll's house made by her father with tiny furniture and electric lights, to frozen water in wintry Norfolk.

The war came frighteningly close to Patsy's family when the ship bound for Hong Kong, on which they were returning to her father's new tour of duty, was involved in an air raid. It was 10th June and Italy had just come into WWII; the ship was then commanded to sail via South Africa.

The War began to separate the family. Because of the new concern about the situation in the Far East all the wives and children going to Hong Kong were ordered to disembark on arrival at Cape Town. Her father had to sail on alone only to find that his posting was later changed to Singapore and his family could have been with him after all! Patsy tells us how comforted she felt when her mother told her about the 'silver cord' that bound the family together however far they were apart and which could never be broken. What a wonderful image of how we are joined to God and the people we love, no matter what are our external circumstances.

Eventually the family were able to be reunited in Singapore, but soon the bombing of Pearl Harbour and Penang brought the War terrifyingly close and it was when on a ship enabling her mother, sister and herself to escape from the Japanese invasion of Malaya that Patsy had a dream of walking in utter peace and safety because Jesus was holding her by the hand. The impact of this dream was never to leave her and became the foundation stone in her life – even when her father was incarcerated in a Japanese Prisoner of War Camp. Patsy writes movingly of that terrible time and also of 'The Malayan Emergency' through which she met the love of her life, her husband, Hugh. Patsy and Hugh lived in Macau before moving to Malaya where their daughter Sheila was born, followed by their twins, Frances and Anna. They finally returned to England and settled in Kent; when working in London, Hugh practised law.

Patsy was only five years old when she first heard the wonderful news of how Jesus died for us. She clearly remembers sitting on the loo and praying, "I am really sorry that people have been so cruel to you, Lord Jesus, because you are so loving, and I want to make this up to You for the rest of my life." I know from personal experience of years of friendship with Patsy that this wonderful prayer has been fulfilled in her generous and self-giving life!

This book is well worth reading so get started quickly, but be warned: you won't want to stop!

Jennifer Rees Larcombe
June 2013

Preface

Mother used to love making up tales for my sister and me, one of which was that before we were born she had had ten other little girls. They were each named after flowers: Rose, Violet, Poppy, Iris, Petunia, Marigold are some I recall. However, I soon became suspicious when I noticed that there were several versions of these names and that various important details about all these older sisters kept changing! But it was an intriguing thought, that we could have had all these unknown sisters, and I found this such fun and enjoyed these stories very much!

When starting to write 'my story' I realise that each of my 'other siblings', had they not been fictitious, would have had a different version, different memories and ways of expression and could quite likely have had much to add – or even to disagree with! So I need to point out that I can only tell what *I* experienced and remember and that my tale is as accurate as possible and is unique to me!

It's alright now – God is in charge!

CHAPTER ONE

To Start at the Very Beginning

To start at the very beginning I will tell about my parents and their meeting many years before I was born!

The young couple noticed each other very shortly after starting to work at the Hong Kong and Shanghai Bank in London. They were both very good-looking – Ralph Wallace Lee being so handsome and Margretta Sheila Shaw a dark haired 'Irish Beauty'. They were in their early twenties and fell deeply in love, seeing one another as often as possible. After a short romance they became engaged! Now, the bank had a rule that their staff had to be in a position to support a wife should they wish to marry, and this meant that the men needed to be at least thirty years of age. Would their love sustain them through the long years of waiting that lay ahead of them?

Soon Ralph was posted to Hong Kong while Sheila (as she was always known) remained working in London. Sheila lived with her mother in Eynsford, Kent, and would commute from there each day. The young couple wrote frequently to one another, but of course, in those days mail would take several weeks either way, and so letters were not a very satisfactory way of communicating. Sometimes there were misunderstandings which would take much time to resolve and caused some heartache in the meanwhile.

Ralph enjoyed the life in Hong Kong – the spectacular scenery and the comradeship with his colleagues. He enjoyed rugger and tennis and also piano playing.

It's alright now – God is in charge!

One day in about October, 1923, Hong Kong experienced a powerful typhoon. In the Hong Kong and Shanghai Bank mess there was a new father who was anxious to get back to his wife and baby on The Peak. He usually travelled up and down this steep hill by the funicular railway, but owing to the fearsome storm the line was closed. Ralph heard about this sympathetically and offered to accompany Philip up to his home and family. They climbed the many hundreds of steps all the way up to The Peak, being constantly buffeted by hurricane-like winds, holding tightly onto any railings, sometimes clutching on to each other for extra support, and coping too with the screeching, deafening sounds of a violent tropical storm. Eventually they reached the house; Ralph was given hospitality by Philip's wife, Margie, and met Hugh, their six month old baby, and his older brother, Richard, then aged about three. This incident became very important in our families many years later!

After the usual five years on tour, Ralph returned to England on leave in 1928 and there was great joy in seeing his beloved again. Then his next posting was to Kobe, Japan, and there were many love-sick letters to his dearest girl, longing to be able to marry her. At last this was possible, and his lovely fiancée, Sheila, travelled out happily for the wedding, which took place on 5th November, 1932. They had been engaged for about ten years so it was quite a big adjustment for them both. There were some wonderful letters written by the blissful bride to her mother, describing the wedding and their joy.

Sheila had lived in Kobe as a child when her father, Francis Shaw, had been an engineer working on some big project. She tells of an amusing story about her brother, Jim, who was talking with another youngster, the Bishop's son. They discussed the work their fathers did, and when Jim explained that his father was a "dam engineer", the Bishop's son was suitably impressed! Afterwards (I think around 1910) Sheila's family returned to Ireland, where they both had roots, and Francis started a new business with the latest motorcars.

Ralph and Sheila returned to England in time for the birth of their first child. They settled in Eynsford, Kent, to be near a delighted grandmother (always known as 'Gan-Gan'), who had written a lovely letter on hearing of an expected baby: "Perhaps this will be one of the two girls you always wanted!" Much to everyone's surprise, this 'baby' turned out to be twins – identical twin girls! After much

14

thought and earnest discussion, they were named Alicia Lindsey (the eldest) and Patricia Margretta. We were christened in St Martin's Church, Eynsford, where I have seen our names in the Baptismal Roll – Lindsey's at the bottom of a page and mine at the top of the next one. We were born in Blackheath, part of Kent in those days, and to my great pleasure this also shows clearly that we are Kentish Maids! It gives me a feeling of having roots! My mother's sister, Aunt Penny (whose real name is Patricia and after whom I am named), is my beloved godmother, and so too is a cousin of my father's, Marian Knight. Lindsey is a family name on my father's side and Alicia is one of the names of my maternal grandmother, her full name being Anna Alicia Augusta; she was very pleased with all her 'A's! Lindsey's godmothers were great friends of Mother's – Kit Pennell, wife of the captain of the ship taking Scott of the Antarctica to the South Pole, and Bertha Haggart, a well-known pianist.

The next posting was to Ipoh in Malaya, and Ralph and Sheila, taking their young daughters, soon settled into their new home. Some months later, Mother was not at all well with tuberculosis, and poor little Lindsey had a serious fall, which caused a worrying injury. It was decided that it would be best for Mother, being so ill, and Lindsey, in great need, to return to England for appropriate treatment. Father engaged an excellent nurse to take care of his family on the voyage and for the following months as necessary. Cables flew between Mother and Gan-Gan; an ambulance was arranged to take Lindsey straight to Great Ormond Street Hospital and transport for Mother to go to a TB Sanatorium. The nurse continued to take care of me with Gan-Gan and Penny's loving assistance.

Eventually, with Lindsey fully recovered and Mother well again, it was possible for us to return to Ipoh and to rejoin Father. This had been a difficult time for Father financially, and as well as missing his family he had cut down severely on expenses with very little social life and no pleasant alcoholic drinks or tobacco.

It's alright now – God is in charge!

From left to right – Lindsey, Mother and Patricia

My first memory ever was in Ipoh. It was on a hot tropical afternoon and I, aged about three, was up from my afternoon rest and having tea in the shade of a wide, spreading tree in the garden of the Bank House. I was leaning against the knee of my mother, sleepily listening to adults' peaceful conversation, the clinking of cups and the pouring of tea.

Suddenly, we saw the summerhouse moving! How could this be? But then I could see legs, many legs, moving swiftly in the manner of men carrying heavy loads, rhythmically, working together, quite fascinatingly like a centipede! A ridiculous scene – which I ran out to see, running alongside this incredible sight, amused beyond words, and laughing hilariously. I remember also, harsh under bare feet, the crisp, broad-leaved grass, the sun hot on my head and the contrast of sun's heat after the shady tree.

Apparently the summerhouse was being moved from one site to another within the huge grounds. "Careful, Missie, keep out of our way," and I, still giggling merrily but ever cautious so as not to be hurt, obeyed the Kebun (the gardener) with alacrity. The little house was gently lowered into its new position, and men appeared from underneath, hot, sweaty and relieved, their toil accomplished with great satisfaction. So I've always remembered this summerhouse marching – and how I was so astonished!

Penny had been invited to join us in Ipoh and eagerly accepted, enjoying being able to help with her twin nieces and looking forward to seeing Malaya. This would have been in 1936 to 1937, when we would have been between two and three years old. Our young and beautiful maiden Aunt Penny had very attractive, curly, auburn hair, a perfect complexion, grey-green eyes and a delightful sense of fun; we all adored her. She was popular with the young men too!

One of these friends, whose work as an ethnologist brought him into contact with some of the aboriginal tribes in Malaya, the Sakai people, invited her and another young girl to join him on a rafting expedition organised by Pat Noone. In those days, when it was customary to have chaperones, two other ladies were also invited.

There were two rafts on this expedition, each manned by strong and experienced aborigine men. As the party set off the ladies were conscious that taking part in the expedition was a rare privilege. The river flowed through the jungle, the only highway in a remote area.

Although they were skilfully handled, the rafts at times would plunge terrifyingly, even riskily, over the rapids as the party swept downstream. The views of the jungle on either side of the river were remarkable, the trees pressing urgently, right to the very edges; in several places branches reached overhead with such a tangle of creepers that any further glimpses were obscured. The scents from the dense jungle were fascinatingly varied, some so sweet and some atrocious. There was a kaleidoscope of colour and a cacophony of sound; it was a memorable excursion in a multitude of ways.

The party landed at a small clearing on the river bank. The nights were spent in aborigine 'long-houses' on stilts, which were usually built near the river's edge. There were compartments in the long-house with mosquito nets. Here, amongst other fascinating things, the evening commenced with Sakai men dancing to the beating of drums by the women, the men becoming more and more excited until they appeared to be in a trancelike state. My aunt found these displays rather frightening and was thankful when they were over. But the rest of the experience was marvellous, and she enjoyed it all – that is, apart from the toilet arrangements. These were very primitive – so she told us, seeming slightly embarrassed – you had to go into the jungle, where there was a hole in the ground covered over by three rough planks! After several days of this wonderful adventure Penny was grateful to get back to civilisation!

When visiting another friend's house she did not enjoy his pet monkey who had the run of the house and snatched their drinks and was into everything! She remembered clearly that he was a real nuisance!

She was also invited to see a tiger being shot at a kill. She was warned she would be required to climb a tree and sit up all night if necessary. "You must not talk," she was told firmly by this friend, a game-warden, George. The young man thought she would enjoy watching for the tiger with him. This particular tiger was a potential threat to a nearby village; it was expected to return to its kill, hopefully before dawn. The unusual invitation came at the close of a most delightful and energetic evening of dancing, but on this occasion she declined the offer and then, always, regretted her decision. She felt, however weary she was and how possibly inconvenient it was, it was an opportunity she should not have missed. Certainly such a chance never came her way again.

When we were older we would love to hear about Penny's adventures; she seemed to have so many and was such fun. She was also very artistic and enjoyed painting several attractive watercolours while out in Malaya, some of which I have on my walls and very much appreciate. There is one of a scene in the Cameron Highlands of a garden of the house we were staying at in Ringlet when my parents were having some local leave. There is a lawn with trees rising up the hillside, behind which are mountains, and (I suppose at about this time) a photo was taken of my sister and me, aged three, with an amah (our help) in the same place. I was pleased and surprised when I found this photograph one day and was able to match it with Penny's painting. I also have a lovely little painting of hers with a view of Kedah Peak as seen from Penang Hill, which again I greatly treasure.

Mother and Penny, on another occasion, were staying at the Cameron Highlands Hotel, when they had an alarming adventure. Many years later when I had returned to Malaya after leaving school, Mother reminded me of this exciting story, retelling it with enthusiasm. We were quietly sitting together after a tiring shopping expedition in Kuala Lumpur, waiting for the refreshing drinks, just requested, to be served. Having gratefully accepted her whiskey and soda drink, known as a 'stengah', Mother leaned comfortably back in the rattan chair, allowing the ice to tinkle musically against the rim of the elegant cut glass tumbler. As she sipped her 'stengah' she began to relax, enjoying the sun-downer on the peaceful hotel verandah. We agreed that a long, cool drink was a perfect way to recover after such an exhaustingly hot day. Mother suddenly laughed and said she remembered another time when she had needed a medicinal drink urgently.

"When you were just a toddler, your Aunt Penny and I were staying at the hotel near the golf links in the Cameron Highlands. We were relaxing in the peace and beauty of the lovely resort. One day we went for a walk together up the hills behind our hotel. This was a rather wild part with jungle growing thickly on the steep slopes; it was a good place for bird watching, a hobby we both enjoyed. We were delighted with the many varieties of the birds in the Highlands and kept looking at the little book which we had brought with us, feeling thrilled whenever we could identify a new bird. We were particularly excited about the weaver-birds we had not seen before. We listened quietly to all the birdsong and admired the scenery glimpsed occasionally through the trees. Soon we found ourselves approaching a large house, the Sultan's holiday home, and paused briefly to have a look at it. As we climbed the hill behind the opulent residence we remarked indignantly to each other, 'Really, these drains smell appallingly. Surely the people here should do something about it; it is most disagreeable!'

"Then, suddenly, from right beside us, unseen in the denseness of the jungle, we heard a tremendous roar. It was some large animal with a very loud and horrible sound. We both immediately thought, with terrified glances at one another, 'Surely, surely not a tiger?' and each of us realised that the quickest way to return to the hotel was to go first towards this petrifying noise as silently and as swiftly as possible. Tightly clasping each other's hands, we hurried back, stumbling down the little path, panic stricken and gasping, to the safety of the hotel.

"On our arrival we collapsed on to the verandah chairs and ordered stiff drinks rather urgently. A man nearby noticed our agitation and enquired kindly, 'Are you ladies all right? You seem a bit anxious.'

"Breathlessly we told him how we had heard this startlingly loud roar so close to us up on the hills behind the hotel. 'Do you suppose it could have been a tiger?' we asked nervously.

"'No,' he replied reassuringly, 'No, it couldn't have been a tiger; because,' he added thoughtfully, 'if you had been as near as that you would have smelled an extremely unpleasant odour, something like very bad drains.'

"Penny and I exchanged horrified looks, and each thought of the other sister that she had never seen anyone who was actually as white as a sheet before! Those medicinal drinks were absolutely necessary to recover our tongues, our colour and our composure!"

———————————

Father was next posted to Penang. Our new home was a very pleasant bungalow on Penang Hill, called 'Aloha', reached by the funicular railway. One of the main events I remember here was of going to a little school and having empty desks but not having anything to put into them, how Lindsey and I both decided we must have something and found things from the garden there – sand and leaves, anything to fill the space!

I wanted so much to learn to read and loved looking at Mother's books, being so pleased when I could read the title 'IF' on one of Amy Carmichael's books! I don't think we went to a church (there probably was not one near enough) but Mother always prayed with us and told us Bible stories.

I recall having measles quite badly, having our rooms darkened and being taught the game played with fingers, "Fly away Peter (or Paul), come back Peter (or Paul)" I also remember being coaxed to eat more as we were recovering. Mother would stuff a potato chip with peas, saying, "Here is a little boat filled with people, and now it needs to go down a river, so open your mouth wide, here it comes..." I can't remember at all if this was swallowed, but it was fun!

I particularly remember our kind amah teaching us to tell 'left' and 'right'. Mother always knew 'port' and 'starboard' but had a great problem with 'left' and 'right' and wanted us to be quite sure about this. The amah took my sister and me for a walk along the road near our house. I clearly remember her saying, 'Now, if you look up to the trees on your *left* you will see a monkey' – and I did; it was such a simple and unforgettable way to learn!

I used to love watching Father prepare fruit for his breakfast. He was so skilful in cutting the peel in one continuous piece; it was fascinating to see. He was obviously creative and worked on making a wonderful doll's house; it looked amazing with little electric lights and tiny furniture; however we were not allowed to play with it, just to look very carefully! I think he was such a perfectionist it would have been a disaster if anything had been spoilt! I believe he was making it for us really but, perhaps, to be given to us only when it was completed to his satisfaction.

There was a spectacular landslide while we were staying at this house, exposing the foundations of the dining room which then hung over the space beneath alarmingly. The huge amount of earth plunged onto the tennis court below and crushed our little pedal cars.

It's alright now – God is in charge!

Sometime after this and, alas, before the doll's house was completed, Father's Home Leave was due and we returned to England, a trip which was sure to have been on one of the P&O liners. We sailed from Singapore, first visiting a Chinese dentist who had beautiful and fascinating goldfish in a tank, and going to someone's party with hired Fraser and Neave slides and swings, wearing brand new white sandals. I also have a hazy memory of the ship calling at Tunis and not being allowed ashore, and feeling indignant that now I might never see Tunis!

Chapter Two

England (Home Leave)

We returned to England from Malaya just before the winter of 1939/40, soon after the outbreak of World War II. We stayed very happily with Gan-Gan and Aunt Penny at Garden Cottage, Necton in Norfolk. I was five years old, and after the tropical heat of the Far East it seemed bitterly cold; the freezing temperatures made quite a big impression, and I particularly recall some wintry incidents.

There was much concern when my mother had an alarming skid somewhere in the country, a nasty experience in snow and ice, but then there were such thanks when all was well.

One night I was thirsty and Mother offered me water from a glass on the windowsill beside my bed. She could not understand when I complained that I was not getting anything to drink, but in the morning we found that the water was completely frozen!

Another vivid memory of that sub-zero winter was when Penny took us 'skating' on a nearby pond. On the walk back to the Cottage in howling, freezing winds, she opened her winter coat, drew me into it and, with it still open, shielded me while I peeped through a button hole, feeling safe and protected. How I loved her for that!

There was an open fire in the sitting room that Gan-Gan used to enjoy lighting. This was quite a rigmarole and I loved to watch the proceedings. Having laid crumpled newspaper in the iron cradle she would carefully lay the kindling and larger pieces of firewood on and around it and then light the crushed newspaper, blowing it as hard as she could. Next she would open a fresh sheet of newspaper and hold it over the top half of the open fireplace to create a better draft, being careful not to let this catch fire too. This was always called an 'Oh My', and I could see why, once when this paper caught fire! It was a scary yet exciting event and certainly "Oh, My!" cried out in alarm seemed just the right response!

A tradition I also enjoyed was when Gan-Gan wound the little carriage clock kept on the mantelpiece and set it to the exact time according to the radio. The clock had been a wedding present; it was French and very precious to her. Later my Aunt Penny inherited it, and to my delight I now have it and really treasure it too.

Another interesting ritual was feeding the birds every day with breadcrumbs sprinkled on the snow over the cover of the old well at the front of the cottage, discovering with joy that they liked our crumbs! I loved the robins but it was the beautiful blackbird with its vivid yellow beak which attracted me most of all.

The Blackbird

Gleaming snow,
Sparkling white,
Tiny blackbird,
Feathers shining,
Yellow beak –
Startling bright!
What a sight
In brilliant light
To remember
With delight!

Penny's 'adventures' included stories about tigers, which she loved to tell to her eager nieces. One of these was about a tiger she saw and another was about one she heard – we would beg her to tell of these adventures again and again. Lindsey and I enjoyed a little ritual early in the morning. We would hop into Penny's bed and beg for 'Tiger Stories'. Sweetly and sleepily she would begin with the time-honoured phrase, "Once upon a time..." We would wriggle happily with anticipation, but with any slight pause in her story telling we would cry, "And then? And then?" encouraging her eagerly. Much to our delight she always warmed to the retelling of tales.

Our favourite tiger story was about when she was driving to Ipoh from the Cameron Highlands in Malaya where we were all on holiday. My father lent her his car (she thought it was a Hillman Minx). She was quite excited about that but was also feeling very responsible for this cherished vehicle.

She told how she had been invited to a St Andrew's Ball at the Ipoh Swimming Club some sixty miles away and went bravely on her own. First, she had to negotiate forty miles of very twisty road, sculptured skilfully into the steep mountainsides. There were hardly any other vehicles on this long descent of six thousand feet. The precipitous mountain slopes were thickly covered by jungle in a multitude of greens; little sparkly streams gushed from waterfalls and plunged into the valleys far below. Gibbons whooped unseen amongst the dense growth of trees and many birds called melodiously to one another. She quietly appreciated the peace of this spectacular scenery, beginning to feel more confident about driving the unfamiliar car.

But, suddenly, she thought she might have a puncture; the steering seemed a little strange. She parked as far to the side of the narrow road as possible, and getting out of the car she anxiously checked each of the tyres. However, all seemed well so she gratefully returned to the driver's seat and was about to start up the engine and to return to the road.

"And then," she would continue the story, with excitement mounting in her voice, "I saw a tiger lying on a rock just beyond where I had stopped the car; he was looking straight at me. I met his eyes – and my knees turned to jelly! I had no choice but to drive past him. I saw him rise to his feet and then he disappeared; he completely disappeared into the jungle trees. But – would he suddenly reappear ready to attack me at the very next bend, would he jump onto the roof of the car? I was terrified, but I just had to go on driving! With my knees still feeling like jelly, I cautiously steered round the bend of the road and... *no,* he was not there!" At this point my sister and I would breathe a sigh of relief – what a near thing! Fancy being so perilously close to that terrible tiger!

On the same day, in the evening, when enjoying the Ball, she told her friends about the tiger. There were mixed reactions; one man commented somewhat enviously, "You've only been in this country what seems half-an-hour and you've seen a tiger; I've been here twenty years and have never seen one at all!" A girl said, "My arms have come out in shivery goose pimples at the very thought!" Others were astonished that she should have had such a close encounter with a very dangerous creature and were surprised at her apparent calmness.

Penny would describe this tiger as being very beautiful with wonderful colouring. She was amazed at how perfectly he blended into the background of the jungle. Thinking about this incident later, she seriously considered what would have happened if she had seen the tiger before she had got back into the car. With her 'knees turned to jelly' she wondered if she could have managed returning to it in a hurry. My dear Aunt Penny would shudder at the thought of possible disastrous consequences for a long time to come!

She once had heard that someone had had the frightening experience of a tiger jumping onto his car and remaining on the roof – perhaps too afraid to jump off as it was moving? It stayed on until they reached a town, but she never knew what had happened next! That story had flashed through her mind!

Penny was reassured once that if you had net curtains at your bungalow windows you could be sure that a tiger would never jump through because it needed to see where it was going to land. She hoped that this would never have to be put to the test!

Such stories would long be remembered and enjoyed.

Later my poor sister, Lindsey, wasn't well and had to have a tonsillectomy at the local hospital in Swaffham. Everything seemed a bit strange and rather unpleasantly different for a while, especially as I didn't understand quite what was happening and was a bit worried. My father enjoyed jigsaw puzzles and would leave unfinished ones on a table, adding pieces to it every now and again; I loved seeing how the picture would gradually grow, and this was somehow reassuring to me at this point.

We were so happy at Garden Cottage, especially when the garden emerged after all the snow; it was a lovely place to play with its little paths edged with pungent scented box hedges. It actually had been built as the garden cottage for Necton Hall, a magnificent house, nearby, and had a beautiful walled garden of about an acre, attractively laid out with paths and large beds for vegetables. Fruit trees were trained against the sunniest walls; apples, pears and even peaches were grown successfully. Surrounding this area beyond the walls there were large greenhouses, potting sheds and many intriguing places to explore including an old ice-house where the apples were stored with their pleasant and distinctive smell.

The adults often listened to the news and there was a great deal of discussion about the outbreak of war and also about the new King and Queen; most of this went over my head, but I realised there were concerns. Gan-Gan had a special mug commemorating the accession of Edward who would once have been king, and I remember being puzzled about some of the things they said.

The baker, with his horse and cart, used to call regularly, coming jerkily along the rough lane from Necton Village, and we also loved the friendly postman, Percy, with his wobbly false teeth, arriving on his ancient bicycle. One day Percy brought a parcel from our paternal grandmother, 'Granny'; on eagerly opening it we found beautifully knitted pink or blue little outfits for our dolls! That was such a joyful surprise, and I remember feeling really known and loved!

It was at Garden Cottage that I vividly remember Gan-Gan telling us how Jesus had died on the cross for us. My five-year-old mind had difficulty in understanding everything that she told me about Jesus, of how and why he had died for us all. But she must have explained it clearly as I understood quite a lot, although it was only much later that I realised that it was also for *my* sins and forgiveness that Jesus had died. I could see that he is wonderfully loving and kind – but why, I wondered sadly, did anyone want to kill him? This was so hard to comprehend. I puzzled and grieved about his death as I was called to have my bath and prepare for bed. My mother and aunt were running the bath for my sister and me, but first I popped into the lavatory, which was separated by a thin wooden partition from the bathroom. As I sat on the seat I remember saying, "I am really sorry that people have been so cruel to you, Lord Jesus, because you are so loving, and I want to make this up to you for the rest of my life." Then I came skipping back to have my bath with no idea that Mother and Penny had overheard me (as decades later they have each reminded me). I wish that I could say that is just as it has been for me always, but alas, that would not be true!

It's alright now – God is in charge!

The Home Leave was wonderful for my parents; we had seen all the closest members of the family, particularly both my grandmothers and two dear aunts. My paternal grandmother lived in Watford, so later on, in the Spring, we rented a pleasant house to be fairly near her and enjoyed our visits to her home. Our rented house had a pretty garden in which there was a small piece of woodland, and I remember liking going to the little school nearby. Here we had brightly coloured crayons, lots of books, and it was great fun doing various gymnastic exercises.

Gan-Gan and Penny came for a visit over Easter, and sitting in pleasantly warm sunshine in the garden, Gan-Gan carefully explained the meaning of Easter eggs.[1] I thought it was a wonderful idea – not just the chocolate(!) but the thought of the way it demonstrated how Jesus burst out of the tomb, fully alive, on Easter Day!

One day Mother took Lindsey and me to see The Wizard of Oz, our very first visit to a cinema! I loved it; best of all was the Fairy Queen, who reminded me of Penny with her beautiful red hair! My parents also took us to Whipsnade Zoo. At some point we excitedly travelled by the Underground, but I distinctly recall the huge disappointment in not seeing the worms in their little homes or any rabbits in their burrows! However, there was much to see and admire at the zoo with so many animals; most of all I loved a little wild rabbit which had found its way into an area by mistake and was enchanting! I was impressed too with the wonder of gliders skimming effortlessly in the sky, as seen from the high hills surrounding the zoo.

Father developed a nasty cold while staying in this rented house, and lost his voice. Not being allowed any closer, I peeped over the footboard of his bed to chat to him. He just managed to speak in a hoarse whisper, and naturally I whispered my reply; he was not at all amused and surprised me by his obvious annoyance. It seemed extraordinary that he could only whisper! A little later I caught the cold and felt quite ill, unable to breathe easily. Father was very kind to me, and I was awed at the way he took such care of me, suggesting that I slept on the sofa in the sitting room and then sleeping on chairs in a makeshift bed in order to look after me! I was deeply impressed and felt so loved.

[1] I have very warm memories of Gan-Gan as a special person in my life, knowing her as the one who introduced me to Jesus in such a real way!

28

My father's sisters, Aunty Joyce with her children, John and Hilary, and Aunty Peggy with her children, Jim and Margaret, came to visit us. We knew our cousins John and Hilary a bit but did not know Jim and Margaret. I hate to confess but I did not like the latter much because they seemed so rough with a particular celluloid parrot I was fond of; they just didn't seem to realise it was precious!

We liked visiting Granny; she thought of interesting things for us to do. One day she suggested that we helped her to make a cake, telling us the various ingredients we would need – this included flour. Being very inexperienced, I remember hurrying into the garden to pick some flowers and being quite embarrassed when I realised this was not what was meant at all! I expect the cake was delicious but I have no recollection of that!

Father enjoyed taking us for walks; some of these were really quite long, I think perhaps several miles, and I remember Mother being concerned about this when we returned home later than she expected, quite weary, and once or twice, surprisingly, by train.

People were talking a lot more about the War, about Hitler, Poland, battles and gas masks, and one day Father insisted we should learn about how to use gas marks in case this should ever be necessary. So, having obtained some, he carefully showed us what to do, making it sound very important and explaining that everyone in England would have their very own mask. This made wearing these uncomfortable contraptions much more acceptable!

However, all too soon Father's leave was completed and thoughts turned to the voyage out to the Far East and his next posting.

CHAPTER THREE

SS Narkunda

*F*ather's leave had come to an end, and it was time to return to his work in the Hong Kong and Shanghai Bank, where he was to serve in Hong Kong itself. The family embarked on the *SS Narkunda* at Southampton in June, 1940. My memories of the P&O ship Narkunda are fairly vivid. Standing on the quay she seemed huge to me. I was well used to ships and sea voyages by the time I was six years old. The routine, the cabins, the smells, the sailors in their smart uniforms, and the different way of life were just taken in my stride, and I easily accepted all that happened.

However, as we set sail for the Far East, Southampton was beginning to suffer an air-raid. The Narkunda had just slipped its moorings and was sailing along the Solent and out to open sea. Suddenly the ship shuddered – something had happened! The passengers were shocked and fearful; for a moment everyone was silent, then there was a loud babble of questioning voices, but almost straight away orders came direct from the captain: "Will all passengers proceed immediately to the dining-rooms, taking their lifebelts with them!"

The passengers, nearly all of whom were very concerned and scared, some obediently, some rebelliously, some doubting and questioning still, filed into the huge dining rooms. Parents were instructed to keep their children happy and amused, and everyone was to maintain calm. Uniformed stewards tried to settle everyone comfortably at tables and offered some games to play. The orchestra played continuously and rather loudly. Later on I learnt that this was to drown out the sounds of bombing!

We waited and waited; there was quite a tense atmosphere. My parents played all sorts of games with Lindsey and me to keep us amused. We were at last offered some refreshments; I happily chose to have some cream crackers and was very disappointed to find that these were so dull – no cream at all and quite tasteless! Mother told me much later that it was a help to all the parents in the crowded dining room to have to entertain their children because it kept their minds off the anxiety of not knowing what was happening. Our ship now had to return to her berth in port. Repairs would be necessary; our steering gear was damaged, although this was not known at once.

After several tense hours the ship was given its sailing orders. This must have been about 10th June as Italy had just come into the War and was now an enemy![2] We could not therefore sail through the Mediterranean after all and would have to take the much longer route around the Cape of Good Hope for the Far East; it was a sudden change of plan for the Peninsular and Orient Shipping Line to reschedule.

There was no convoy so we had to zigzag all the way to avoid enemy submarines, the dangerous U-boats lurking in the Atlantic. This made the voyage much longer, but it was a necessary tactic in wartime making any attack more difficult; apparently the enemy needs a maximum target of the whole of a ship's broadside when attacking. We were instructed to keep our lifejackets with us at all times and to be very careful with fresh water as it was in short supply with a longer route than anticipated. We were to only use sea water for baths, and definitely no lights of any kind were to be shown after dark, not even lighted cigarettes.

My parents were very careful to be sure that our lifejackets were with us always, but once Mother told us indignantly that one was missing and that someone, a man, had taken one of ours! However, having noticed this and, importantly, being able to prove it, it was retrieved; extra vigilance was obviously required.

We sailed almost as far as South America, stopping briefly first in the Canary Isles for essential supplies and fuel. We were not allowed

---

[2] Italy declared war on 10th June, 1940.

to disembark – the people were quite hostile to our British ship – but I do remember seeing graceful dancers with their intricate moves on the quayside in Madeira.

Then the news came that France had fallen[3], which of course was heard with dismay and people wondered what they could possibly do. Some French and Dutch people moaned that the hard-hearted English would still go on with their dances, but Mother wondered, "What can we do; it is ridiculous!" "What we did," she later remembered, "was to have the most wonderful church service in which we all prayed, not only for our own safety but for the entire world; it was a very special prayer and everyone seemed to join in wholeheartedly, not just singing hymns but really praying. It was... well, never to be forgotten!"

In spite of the men being required to take on 'lookout duties' because of the danger of German submarines in the Atlantic Ocean, there was a determination amongst the passengers that this voyage should be as normal as possible with all the usual fun and life on board. Ballroom dances still took place, and one marvellously memorable night, Lindsey and I crept out of our cabin to watch the dancers, particularly the ladies in their gorgeous dresses, with such wonderful music! We peeped through the elegant balustrade of the beautiful staircase, thoroughly enjoying the spectacle and every now and again saw Mother dancing on the floor below us, looking magnificent and graceful – we were very proud of her! She was wearing a pink dress which became silvery grey in certain lights. She was an exceptionally beautiful lady with her dark, wavy hair, blue-grey eyes, lovely complexion and bone structure, all of which gave her such strikingly good looks.

At last we arrived at Cape Town. Here it was winter and it seemed cold and grey and uninviting! I do not even remember seeing Table Mountain as I think everything was misty and so dull. But suddenly plans were completely changed! All families travelling to Hong Kong had new orders; wives and children were to disembark, the explanation being that women and children were being evacuated from Hong Kong. As there were fears at that time about a possible war with Japan, no further arrivals would be permitted.

---

[3] France capitulated on 14th June.

You can imagine the turmoil, a sudden adjustment of all plans. Luggage had to be reorganised; there was much anxious discussion; and people had to go to the baggage hold to deal with the trunks and cases, making rapid decisions and repacking almost everything. Then, accommodation somewhere in Cape Town had to be found for us; apparently this was very difficult at this time. But somehow, with great perseverance (as Cape Town was incredibly full of people), my parents found a YWCA Hostel called 'The Towers', in Muizemburg, on the coast at False Bay, which would be able to take us.

It must have been very hard for Father to continue his voyage alone to Hong Kong leaving us in a strange country! And it was not at all easy for Mother either, to find herself in a completely unfamiliar place with two little daughters and on her own without him. It was all so bewildering and unexpected!

Then, well on his way to the Far East, too late he heard that his posting had been altered – he was to disembark at Singapore after all, and *we could have been with him!*

SS Narkunda

I have always been enthusiastic about ships and have found some interesting facts about The Narkunda. I believe that her name was taken from Rudyard Kipling's book 'Plain Tales from the Hills'. She was a passenger liner, built by Caird and Co. in Greenock in about 1920 for the Peninsular and Orient Line (usually known as the P&O), and was to serve the Far East and Australia.

She weighed about sixteen and a half thousand tons, was just over six hundred feet long and almost seventy feet wide. She seemed to me to be very long and not very high when I saw her at the dockside! She had three funnels and two masts – one forward and another nearer the stern. She would have had some six hundred and fifty passengers in first and second class accommodation and only four in third class. (I wonder what that would have been like!)

On the return voyage to Southampton from Australia and the Far East passengers would often disembark at Marseilles to travel overland by train to reach the UK more quickly. On 21st May, 1940, on the voyage just before ours, when the Narkunda arrived there it was found that the special overland train to Paris and the channel coast had been cancelled because of the war situation in France. I can imagine everyone's dismay when they were compelled to go by sea after all! Soon after passing Gibraltar the Narkunda, sailing home to England, was chased by an unknown vessel, which she evaded by steaming full speed ahead and at last was relieved to dock safely at Southampton by the end of the month.

The Narkunda was in the Indian Ocean homeward bound when war was declared on 3rd September, 1939. She had two further voyages without incidents on her usual route, returning to Southampton on 31st May in good time for our departure on 10th June, 1940. This voyage was her last full passenger one scheduled for Hong Kong, however, because Italy declared war just then. She sailed via Cape Town and returned the same way, this time to Liverpool, on 28th October, 1940.

A couple of weeks later she sailed again, taking both passengers (who would have been fare-paying) and troops for the voyage to Penang, Malaya, via Cape Town, and returned safely to Liverpool mid-April. She was then refitted as a troop carrier and served only as such, apart from on three special occasions.

A month before Singapore fell, the Narkunda returned to pick up women and children escaping from the Japanese.[4] Later, on another voyage in July 1942, she was deployed to repatriate British diplomats who were to be exchanged for Japanese diplomats held by the Allies and ordered to call at Lorenzo Marques. The word 'Diplomats' was painted (several feet high) on the hull along with four very large Union Jacks. Because of these special passengers the whole ship was floodlit every night to highlight this fact; this made it a unique voyage in wartime when every light of any sort was totally forbidden!

On 1st November the Narkunda sailed from the UK carrying troops to Algiers as part of the Operation Torch designed to cut off the Axis forces in North Africa. After some of the troops disembarked she sailed on to Bougie on 14th November, where she continued to disembark stores and the remainder of the troops. This took nearly all day; then early in the evening she started to sail homewards. At this point she suffered a fierce air-raid as German bombers attacked; the ship was abandoned and the Narkunda sank

---

[4] I wonder if this was the ship which brought the welcome letter and presents to us in South Africa from my Father, the last we heard from him before he became a P.O.W. – it is a possibility!

by the stern. Thirty-one crew members were killed, but the remainder were able to reach the UK by rescuing ships.

It was wonderful that all the troops on board had already safely disembarked! But this gives some idea of the dangers all shipping suffered during the War. With the Viceroy of India and the Cathay having been lost a few days earlier, the Narkunda became the third P&O liner to be sunk during the North African landings.

CHAPTER FOUR

South Africa – Unexpected!

*T*he YWCA Hostel was such a wonderful answer to prayer, and the warden, Miss Hilary Steynor, was a great help. There was much to learn – new currency, for example. The three-penny bits were called Tikkies (I always liked that!) There were different expressions to get used to, as well as many interesting words and accents. This attractive hostel was situated in a beautiful location, near the sea and just below mountains.

In due course Mother found and rented a flat for us in St James Bay. It was in a block of apartments on the main coast road and had a balcony overlooking this with a lovely view of the sea and the whole of the spectacular False Bay with Simon's Town and the Cape of Good Hope to the west and sweeping round to the east point.

Father was thousands of miles away, and we all missed him very much. Mother would have needed him also to help control his two 'rascals'! Sometimes she would sit in her favourite chair by the window in the flat and draw us both lovingly close to her and remind us of him. We would talk about the things we enjoyed doing together and of the things he might say to us. This was remarkably healing, but the greatest thing of all (to my mind) was that Mother would tell us of the silver cord that always bound every family together, how this cord could never be broken however far away the members were separated from each other. This cord bound our little family safely together, so whatever we did continued to matter to Daddy even though he couldn't be with us! I was thrilled to think that we mattered so much to him and that he always loved us even from that distance! She would encourage us to pray for him. Looking back, I believe that these ideas showed Mother's wisdom; they not only kept us together but were a great way in helping to discipline us!

She also found a school for us. It was within walking distance. It was not a very happy place for me, and I did not like it. There were so many unfamiliar things to adjust to and I know I struggled. I did like the music lessons though, when we were given various percussion instruments and had fun shaking or banging them!

One day, at home, Lindsey and I were bored and needed entertainment. We thought out an idea, and carefully balancing a bowl of water on the edge of the balcony wall, we surveyed the passers-by on the pavement below our first floor flat. It was quite interesting just watching them all, and then suddenly we both knew at once that our victim was approaching! We'd never seen him before, but surely here was our man; he wore a hat and was striding purposefully along.

With deep concentration we aimed accurately, the water pouring directly onto the hat now immediately below us in a most satisfactory way! We hurriedly vanished below the balcony wall... but began to feel anxious as we heard footsteps coming very firmly up our stone steps. The doorbell sounded loudly with a prolonged ring, and we heard Mother's surprised reply and indignation, then possibly an apology. Not waiting to hear any more we fled in panic to the safety of the large built-in wardrobe. We both quivered amongst Mother's dresses and were beset by appalling giggles.

The man continued on his walk angrily. Mother soon found us and, furious about our dreadful behaviour, scolded us vigorously! She not only reprimanded us but also got us to put ourselves into that man's shoes. We started to understand her point and actually began to feel sorry! Never again did we try that particular way to relieve any boredom!

Another never-to-be-forgotten incident took place a few months later! My sister and I were strictly brought up and were not allowed much in the way of sweets. One day, when passing the sweet shop stall near our school, neither of us could resist the great temptation to snatch a delicious looking lollipop from the stall outside! Then we were terrified; the shop owners made it clear at once that we had been observed! They scolded us vociferously, shouting so raucously that we just fled down the road as fast as we could! But the feeling of guilt is really most uncomfortable! We couldn't return home with our lollipops; Mother was sure to ask where we had got them. We knew we were not allowed to accept sweets from strangers, so now what were we to do? It was such a problem! We decided that the best solution would be to cautiously hide these two attractively wrapped lollipops under a bush by the wall above the pavement, planning to find them the following morning on the way to school and to enjoy them there! The next day we eagerly retrieved our lollipops... *but* there was nothing left inside the bright wrappings except their little sticks. Ants had eaten the entire contents! Such dismay! This actually taught us an important lesson; never did either of us ever succumb to such a temptation again!

Then there was a horrid event at the school when I was accused of 'taking' or 'stealing' some keys. I now knew something about stealing – and the very unpleasant guilty feeling that accompanied it! But this false accusation made me most upset; the keys were nothing to do with me, and I could not understand what they were talking about! The only thing that comforted me was that every morning at the School Assembly we used to sing 'There is a Green Hill Far Away' and I found again and again that the words were so real and meaningful – it was amazingly soothing!

Mother then found another school for us, quietly aware of the situation in an understanding way.[5] The next school was very small and took place in a private house. We used to play in the school garden, learning to sing such songs as 'Round and Round the Mulberry Bush', which was quite fun. Here we had to learn some Afrikaans, another new situation which I am sorry to say neither of us liked at all! Why, I remember thinking, did 'sleep' in English (which surely everyone understood) have to be 'slaap' in Afrikaans? I don't think I was a good pupil at all! We did not hear much Afrikaans in those days, and it was sadly unintelligible to us.

But what I really enjoyed was taking a picnic onto the rocks and beach just across the road from our flat. We would have to go through a little tunnel under the railway line, which ran from Simon's Town to Cape Town, to get onto the beach. This was rather

---

[5] I wonder now if there was some anti-British feeling in that school. We certainly experienced this a few years later.

unpleasantly smelly, but we were soon on the beach and having a lovely time, loving the huge waves and the sea and the salty tang of the fresh air.

There was a flight of stone steps outside our flat, which climbed steeply up the mountainside behind us. I was astonished once when Mother spoke about the 'white horses' on the sea; I couldn't even see *one* horse anywhere, until she explained about the enormous waves and the beauty of the foam and spray which were seen clearly from the top of these steps. I have always appreciated 'white horses' ever since! Another vivid memory was of masses of vibrantly colourful nasturtiums growing by these steps. These soon became my favourite flowers; I still love them! It was on these steps once that we had the excitement of seeing an eclipse of the sun. We were only allowed to look through dark brown-coloured glass. It was really fascinating!

I became seriously ill with double pneumonia, a very worrying time for Mother. She employed a lovely Swedish nurse to help look after me. To care for me, Mother shared her room with me, and one of my memories of this time was of Mother kneeling beside her bed praying, with her long plaited hair hanging down her back. As I convalesced, the understanding nurse would often set up a basin with sand, arranging it to look like a little garden, using my favourite flowers, nasturtiums, in their bright colours and a mirror as a pond! I was enchanted by this arrangement! She also gave me a card with a picture of nasturtiums and the printed words, "As for me and my house, we will serve the Lord." I kept this card for a great many years and trusted that this would be true for me one day too.

I believe I was one of the first patients in South Africa to be prescribed M&B medication, and I think this helped me to recover, even if this did take some considerable time.

Mother must have found this a difficult time, being so far from Father, and then she heard that my dear grandmother Gan-Gan had died. I found her sitting sadly on our balcony once and sensed something of the deep grief she felt; I longed to comfort her. I think she may have felt very alone at times and was concerned that we would not know what to do if something happened to her. So she taught us the actions to take if we ever found her lying very still and how to tell if she had died. We were to hold a mirror in front of her face and see if there was any sign of breath on the glass. If we were worried we were to go to neighbours and tell them, and then they would take care of the situation! She had suffered from TB previously and was aware that she wasn't very strong. All her life she said that she would probably die young – actually she lived happily until aged ninety-seven, a dearly loved and greatly respected lady with a delightful sense of fun and humour! She had a deep faith as a Christian, which I always found inspiring.

We did not have many books but there was one I loved particularly. It was a Bible Story Book which had many attractive pictures, but there were some about Jesus' Crucifixion which I could not bear to see; then I would turn the pages quickly, two at a time, so I wouldn't have to look at it. I really hated to think of Jesus' pain and agony. I remember being concerned that Jesus had died and that when He left the earth, did He leave us all too? Mother explained in a way that made a big impression. "No," she said, "He would never leave us, but what happened next was that He gave us all His Holy Spirit and so he would be with us always." "Just think," she continued, "suppose He was still on the earth – how few people would be able to be with Him! But because He died and rose again and then promised to give each one of us His Holy Spirit, how much better that is! You see, now we can all be with Him all the time!" I thought that was marvellous and very reassuring!

Mother was very beautiful and had long, wavy hair, but one day she decided to be fashionable with a new hairstyle; it was not popular with me at all!

This poem was written when I found the old roller she used for her new hairstyle and which evoked strong memories of my feelings!

Hairstyle

No! No, I don't like it,
I don't like it at all!
You are not the same person –
Your hair has grown tall,
I liked the way it used to fall!
You're looking so different,
You're looking so new –
I want a return
To the Mother I knew!

But aren't her voice, and her profile
Her ears, and her nose and her eyes
Just the same – or are they?
Is it just her hair
Without any waves,
All swept up and looking so stiff,
Is that all it is
That makes her so strange?
No! I know, I know very well,
As I can tell, I don't like it a bit!
Where's my Mother...
This one's all changed
And so unfamiliar!
Where's my own Mother,
This one is just similar,
And I'm not going to trust her,
Please, real Mother, return here again!
She's just joking and teasing
And very displeasing!
I've made up my mind,
I think she's unkind
No, it's not suitable,
Nor is it beautiful!
I want my own Mother
I want to be sure,
I need to feel safe,
And very secure!
So away with that hairstyle,
If you say that you're you,
Return to the Mother
That I thought that I knew!

Mother became involved with a group who helped in organisations like the Red Cross. There would be meetings during which tea and sandwiches were served, and while recovering from pneumonia I liked to join in and help too. I was warned to be very careful with a sharp knife, but once, to my horror, I did cut my hand! Much fuss was made and I think both Mother and I were very embarrassed! I also remember being astonished by some of the conversations I overheard. "The Americans talk with a pebble in their mouths; you can hardly recognise what they say!" This would have been said indignantly in, what seemed to me, such a strong South African accent that I had difficulty in understanding *them* sometimes! One very hushed and shocked comment was, "And do you know they dance so close to each other that you couldn't even get a sheet of newspaper between them!" That was quite hard for me to work out!

Mother used to visit the hospital in Simon's Town to see some wounded soldiers or airmen there. We would travel by train, and I remember feeling very sorry indeed for some of these homesick and wounded young men in their lonely hospital beds. Occasionally a very special dog called Nuisance, a Great Dane, would be on our train; he was popular with everyone and we loved to pet him. He used to hop onto trains, and go to Cape Town and other places on the route on his own; he was lovingly allowed to do so by all, being such a character and a real favourite. Much later a striking statue was erected in Simon's Town in his memory!

After almost a year, Mother began to think that she could join Father in Singapore. There did not seem to be any reason not to; there were no further signs of trouble in the Far East as far as she could see, and women and children were already returning to Hong Kong. Father agreed at first and, having prayed about this, Mother felt it was the right thing to do; so she started to make arrangements, managing to book a passage on a Dutch liner on her voyage to Indonesia, sailing from Durban. This meant a long journey for us by train. Finally, when the flat was successfully packed up and various items sold, there was a concerned letter from Father expressing uneasiness. However, all the plans had been made already, so with much more prayer she went ahead with a brief stay at The Towers again before going to the Cape Town mainline station.

To her horror there were huge newspaper headlines on the Cape Town platform telling of impending troubles in the Far East, warning that war with Japan was inevitable! But what was she to do? Again she prayed and felt she was to continue with her arrangements and decided not to let Father know just yet that we were on our way. On arrival at Durban she found that some trouble about her visa had to be sorted out so it was not yet possible to board the ship, but there did not seem to be any accommodation whatsoever; she and her daughters went in search everywhere. It was exhausting! She remembers going into a particular shop and seeing some comfortable sofas, just longing to be able to lie down to have a much needed rest! However, eventually, she found a YWCA hostel and explained her predicament. There was a very kind lady manageress who agreed to take us in. She made a screen with blankets across a lounge, finding a camp bed for Mother and arranging chairs in the shape of beds for us children behind this, giving us some privacy! And we all slept well in our thoughtfully provided beds.

We were able to board our Dutch merchant ship, Tegelberg, the following day. Mother was delighted with the comfortable accommodation we were given on such a luxurious liner. In settling into this cabin she was suddenly overwhelmed with the presence of the Lord – it seemed like a marvellous light enveloping her with deep assurance and love, an amazing experience which she was never to forget in all the times ahead.

There was a very nervous fellow passenger on board, fearful about the voyage, about the enemy submarines in the Indian Ocean, about the future – in fact a very anxious man. Mother tried to reassure him, saying she knew that all would be well, that God was looking after us all. Sadly, this just seemed to make him angry. However, Mother was not going to let anything distress her; she was completely at peace, having a wonderful awareness of the presence and protection of the Lord.

We arrived safely at Batavia[6] and disembarked. We were kindly given hospitality by the Manager of the Hong Kong and Shanghai Bank, and Mother cabled Father to tell him where we were and to ask if we should come to him at Singapore! Much to her joy, he cabled in return, "Delighted. Proceed." Before this she had not felt it right to even discuss with him by letter or cable about her plans!

There was a convenient ship which then took us to Singapore – and a joyous reunion! What a relief to have a father again! It was comforting too, to see him smoking his familiar tobacco pipe with its distinctive aroma! We settled happily into a pleasant hotel, the Sea View Hotel, on the beach just out of Singapore, where we had a chalet type rooms with a small verandah facing the sea. Meals were taken in an attractive dining room that was nearby. My parents found a little school close to the hotel further along the coast and

---

[6] Now called Jakarta

bought a tiny Fiat with an open roof for Mother's use; life seemed to settle down normally at last. We were to stay in the hotel until the house being built for us in a Hong Kong and Shanghai Bank compound, with a group of several others, was completed.

I loved being back in Malaya with its familiar sights, smells and sounds. I liked the amah's wooden clogs and the clacking noise they made when walking. I loved the Singapore Swimming Club where we seemed to spend a great deal of time. I very much liked the 'Eskimo Pie' ice creams which were to be found there always! The high diving board was a real attraction, and it could be difficult for our parents to get us out of the pool at times! But I did not like being stung by a jelly fish when swimming in the sea once; even though people tried to comfort me by pointing out the amazing pattern the red sting mark made on my knee, I just did not appreciate it at all!

Lindsey and I enjoyed playing outside our chalet at the hotel. A huge gun was being installed, and it must have been concreted in firmly because there was some lovely sand for the cement round about which was great fun to play with. I had no real idea then of what the gun could mean.[7]

Father took us once to see his bank office near the harbour in Singapore, and I was most impressed by the size, the jangle of sound with all the typewriters hard at work. I loved the Keppel Harbour with its busyness and endless movement of boats; I was very happy indeed! Except that one day I knew I did not want to go to school. I think this was due to the feeling of tension in the air; people were beginning to be concerned about the growing disquiet over the current situation, and at the school we had to wait with the sun burning hotly on our heads while standing in lines before going into classes. I hid behind the dressing table in our hotel bedroom and, being thoroughly disobedient, disregarded the anxious calls from my parents. Eventually a most worried father found me and scolded me angrily! I was firmly taken to school feeling very chastened. But the wise teacher gave me some nice 'sewing' to do; I was encouraged to use pretty threads to sew on a card with a beautiful picture of tulips!

---

[7] Years later I found that it was a 15" coastal gun which, although facing out to sea, could be turned to fire in other directions and would have been very useful in war with the right ammunition.

After a while Father was due some local leave and planned to take us to a favourite place, the Cameron Highlands in Malaya itself. We had been there quite often before and happily looked forward to this precious time together.

The Tegelberg

This ship was built for Koninklijke Paketvaart Maatschappij of Batavia (usually known as KPM) in 1938, by the Netherlands Shipbuilding Company. She and her two sister ships were to operate the company's route from South Africa to Japan via the Indies (Batavia).

The Tegelberg was about two hundred and sixty feet long and a little more than seventy-two feet wide; the gross Tonnage was 14,500. She had a crew of 231 and could carry some 664 passengers altogether (five hundred of these would be in third class).

In 1942 she was re-fitted as an allied landing ship, serving in the Malayan, North Africa and Sicily landings.

In 1945 she became a passenger liner again, working first with her original owners and then for the new Royal Interocean Lines (RIL) sailing between Japan via Hong Kong, South Africa and South America. She worked on this route until she was sold for scrap in 1968.

CHAPTER FIVE

The Cameron Highlands

What an exciting place! At six thousand feet in the central range of mountains in Malaya, it was cool, beautiful and a wonderful location for holidays. The main resort area was situated around an attractive little valley where there was just enough space for the popular nine-hole golf course. Two hotels were built on the perimeter road encircling the golf course, with many charming houses dotted about, their driveways ascending from this road in varying degrees of steepness. These houses were owned by well-known business firms and banks and much enjoyed by members of their staff for holidays. The jungle, quite dense in parts, grew enticingly behind these buildings up the surrounding hills and were teeming with wildlife.

It was November, 1941, when my father was due some local leave from Singapore where he worked in the Hong Kong and Shanghai Banking Corporation. This was a convenient time because the new house we were to move into was not yet completed and certainly not ready for occupation, so he had arranged to take his wife and twin daughters (we were then aged about seven years) up to the Cameron Highlands to stay in the Bank Bungalows.

We came by train from Singapore as far as Tapah, the railway station at the foot of the hills, where we hired a car for our holiday and for the final forty miles of our long journey, the spectacular climb up to the mountains. The narrow road, skilfully built into the mountainsides, was a continuous series of twists and turns with some dangerously sharp corners to be negotiated very carefully. I enjoyed the attractive little road signs at frequent intervals on this road, warning of dangers and telling drivers to sound their horns. My mother once suggested that Lindsey and I should count the number of bends in one mile, and we found that there were twenty-seven in that particular stretch!

Taken on a previous visit to the Cameron Highlands with our parents when we were about five years old
(Lindsey is on the right)

We wondered where it was exactly that my Aunt Penny had seen a tiger on the roadside a few years earlier, and agreed it would be wonderful if we could see one too. Although it was one of my favourite stories, secretly I knew that I would not like to have quite such a scary encounter!

It's alright now – God is in charge!

The steep mountainside was on our left, with the jungle on our right side, plunging down into deep unseen valleys. I loved the water-falls, hearing the sounds of the cascading rush of rivulets tumbling over rocks, and watching them mysteriously disappearing beneath the road only to reappear again on the other side, before descending with further sound effects, and spray at times, as they leapt down the precipitous hills. We could hear 'wow-wow monkeys' (gibbons) whooping in the trees and see birds swiftly fleeing to shelter as we drove along. The car climbed steadily, with frequent gear changes to take the sharp corners gently, the engine moaning and straining on the steepest parts.

My mother rejoiced over the wildlife and any views she could see, pointing out anything she thought would interest us all. She kept murmuring happily, "Oh, the coolth [one of her favourite expressions!] after the heat of the plains," beginning to feel more alive and able to breathe more comfortably.[8] My father was somewhat stern, concentrating on the difficult driving, but he must have been under considerable pressure for some time, working on two fronts – his demanding work in the Bank during the day and as a volunteer in the Singapore Straits Settlements at night. This holiday was so needed for both my parents.

With increasing delight, we reached the little village of Tanah Rata at last, with its Indian and Chinese shops and a hotel; a couple of miles further on we reached the golf course, where we could see the surrounding mountains with clouds spilling over their peaks. After passing the Cameron Highlands Hotel we turned sharply left, and ascending still further, with yet more twists and turns, we arrived at the Bank Bungalows. Here there was such peace, such stillness and silence after the long drive. The Chinese cook and his wife who worked in the house (the amah) greeted us warmly; they too remembered our previous visit, and we were all very pleased to be back again. We were quickly settled in, the sitting-room fire lit, and after supper my sister and I were soon tucked up in our beds, happy and contented.

These two Bank Bungalows were charming with their English-style thatched or tiled roofs, and roomy accommodation. We were in

---

[8] Many years later, I understood that because she had had tuberculosis, the tropical heat of Malaya seriously affected her.

the lower one, where there was a lovely view of the golf course below and also of the ranges of mountains all around us. The upper Bungalow was reached by a steep flight of stone steps and had a tennis court.

'Our' Bank Bungalow, Cameron Highlands

Father enjoyed his daily golf, although sometimes we would all go for walks together, Father using his walking stick in a particular way, with large vigorous and rhythmical swings. In the evenings he would entertain his daughters, with one of his 'rascals' (as he lovingly called us) sitting on each arm of his chair, drawing pictures and amusing us greatly. My mother joined him playing golf, but occasionally she would take Lindsey and me for delightful walks exploring the quiet little roads carved out of the hillside nearby with steep mossy banks on either side. Here she enchanted us with stories of fairies, showing us where they lived, pointing out their little paths along these banks on a minute scale. Our imagination captured, soon we could also visualise their tiny palaces, their little homes, the meeting places where they danced, and other important fairy things. I loved imagining such different lives. Even now I sometimes pause beside such moss-covered banks and can recapture the enchantment!

It's alright now – God is in charge!

Then, abruptly, our delightful holiday came to a sudden end! All volunteers of the armed forces were mobilized on 1st December (1941), and the men from their various businesses, tin mines or rubber plantations were urgently recalled to their army bases. Being in the Straits Settlement Volunteers Forces, Father had to return to Singapore, and he left at once in the hired car. Nearly every man was in some part of the army, very often in the volunteer forces, so there was a great exodus of men from the Cameron Highlands on that day. It was rumoured that the negotiations between the American and Japanese governments had broken down in Washington, and it seemed that war might be imminent.

As everyone thought it would be best if wives and children remained on the Hill, Mother invited two friends, who had been staying in Government accommodation, to move into our large bungalow. So Eileen Rix (a doctor whose husband was on a course in India) with her two sons, an amah and a golden cocker spaniel, and Kathleen (a nurse) with her son and daughter all moved in with us. Eileen had a little Austin 7 car, which was a help to us all. Both Eileen and Kathleen were working at the local hospital, helping in its preparations, just in case there would be any need or casualties, because the Cameron Highlands would be good place for convalescing. Kathleen's husband was a surgeon working in a hospital further north at Alor Star, on the west coast.

Mother took care of all the children while Eileen and Kathleen were out during the day. We children, all aged about seven years, had great fun together. I remember one occasion particularly when it was raining very heavily; we each had an umbrella and, defying the elements, thoroughly enjoyed the feeling of being dry and secure beneath our Malayan 'payongs', the rain sounding terrific, pattering noisily on the oiled paper! I remember vividly the distinctive smell and the cane workings of these attractively crafted umbrellas, which were so cheap and practical that nearly everyone used them.

My parents were in touch with each other as much as possible by telephone, but this was difficult with the long hours Father had to work both daily at the bank and at night training with the volunteers. Kathleen's husband would phone from his hospital, and she was surprised when he seemed to be on the move; he was gradually coming southwards from one hospital to another. When she asked about this, his rather evasive reply was, "It seems a good idea! I will let you know if anything serious happens."

On 7th/8th December, 1941, the Japanese attacked Pearl Harbour, the American Naval Base in the Pacific. There was now tremendous concern. The Americans joined the Allies, and war was declared on the Japanese! In those days Europeans were fairly complacent, content to know that the guns in defence of the naval base were facing out to sea and would surely defeat any invasion from the sea by the Japanese. It was said that Singapore was invincible!

On 10th December the two British battleships Repulse and Prince of Wales were both sunk by Japanese aircraft off the east coast of Malaya, with a tragic loss of life. There was now great consternation; this was really horrifying news. These warships had been sent by Churchill to bolster the naval defence of Singapore, and the people there had had such confidence in this powerful addition to their protection.

On 11th December Penang was bombed by the Japanese. Many local people were so naive and unsuspecting that when they heard the low flying aircraft they ran out into the streets to see what was happening and were killed in their hundreds.

Kathleen's husband phoned again from the hospital at Ipoh[9], saying, "We have now moved to Ipoh. You are not to worry; there is nothing to worry about. We are holding the Japs; all is well!"

The sound of shelling and the thuds of exploding bombs, perhaps from Ipoh, could be heard even in the mountains, probably by being echoed by the clouds. I am not sure whether my mother and her friends realised this then; it was only later that they understood what this unusual noise was. In order not to damage morale very little news about the actual facts of the Japanese invasion was given over the radio. That people in those days had almost no information is

---

[9] Ipoh is only thirty miles as the crow flies from the Cameron Highlands and six thousand feet below, on the plains.

quite hard for us to understand now with our mobile phones, internet and instant television pictures! The fact was that the Japanese Army had started to invade Malaya from Siam in the north, and our troops were being forced to withdraw steadily southwards.

The situation was growing more serious every day, but my mother and her friends, as well as everyone else in the Cameron Highlands, were disgracefully uninformed of the truth. The day soon came when they were all in for a terrible shock! The significance was not then fully understood, but life would never be the same again for any of us!

CHAPTER SIX

Helter-skelter

other and her friends tried to continue their lives as normally as possible. They heard very little of what was happening far away on the lowlands of Malaya but were becoming increasingly uneasy. Surely it was rather odd that Kathleen's husband seemed to be moving southwards to different hospitals so often, and what did he mean by saying there was no need to worry, that they were holding the Japs? The wives talked these things over, but with no real information it was difficult to know what they could do, so Eileen and Kathleen drove off every day to the hospital as usual, and Mother continued to take care of the children.

Then a friend of Eileen's suddenly arrived at the Bank Bungalows. She lived in the northern part of Malaya but owned a house in the Cameron Highlands. She had come in a great hurry to collect some things from it; when she saw Eileen and the others she was extremely worried. "My dears," she said, tense with anxiety, "look at my car and see those bullet holes! The Japanese fired at me as I left home; the British soldiers waited for me to cross the river before they blew up the bridge, then there were snipers firing at me too!"

The wives felt it was very alarming, but what could they do? However, a day or so later following this incident, after the others had left for their work in the morning, my mother had a phone-call. It was about the 16th December. My father was on the line (that much she realised) but all she could hear on the very poor connection was the word, "NOW!"

"What do you mean by 'now'?" she enquired anxiously. Again, just the word "NOW!" came over – loud, insistent, and sounding extremely urgent. It was an appalling line! "Do you mean that you want us to come to Singapore now?" she asked, recognising the urgency in my father's voice. The reply was an immediate, emphatic "YES!" – then the line went dead.

Mother, praying hard, went thoughtfully out into the garden and looked down at the golf course; to her amazement, she realised that there was no one to be seen! The course, usually so full of people either playing golf or meeting one another with children skipping about, showed no sign of any life whatever. Just at that moment there was the sound of tyres on the gravel driveway as the little Austin 7 spun round the corner; Eileen and Kathleen had returned and hurried breathlessly out of the car, pale with anxiety, saying, with near panic in their voices, "There are no Europeans left on the Hill; we should have gone too! Everyone else was evacuated early this morning! All the other people have gone long ago by their own vehicles or buses, and lorries have already come to each house to collect all their possessions and luggage. [10] We must all go immediately!" The words came tumbling out; they were both in a state of shock.

They all realised that they must get away at once, but what could they do with just one small car? Eileen offered to take the six children to Kuala Lumpur. Mother, still praying constantly, hesitated for a moment and decided that it would not be right to be parted from her children and that somehow she and her girls would find their own way down from the Cameron Highlands. There was no time to argue; it was now known clearly that the Japanese Army had invaded Malaya and was rapidly making its way southwards.

---

[10] For some reason, when the District Officer in the Cameron Highlands was informing everyone in all the houses on the Hill to leave at once and was making any necessary arrangements for their transport and luggage, our house had not been contacted, and we had been left unaware of the order to evacuate! Decades after this incident Hugh and I had the privilege to meet this very man when he came to stay with us! We all spoke about our days in Malaya, and to our astonishment, we heard that our new friend had been the District Officer in the Cameron Highlands at that time! He apologized! - Though of course it would have been one of the staff who should have contacted us about the urgent evacuation.

Mother went straight to the telephone and rang number after number – the taxis, the hotels, anyone who might be able to help with transport to take us down to the Station at Tapah – but there were no replies at all. Nothing! It was such a weird sensation; where were all these people?

Mother, now in our bedroom, quietly packed a small cane suitcase with a few necessities. Then seating herself in a wicker chair, she called Lindsey and me to her, saying gently, "Darlings, we are in trouble and we really need God to help us. There is a promise that Jesus made that if two of you on earth agree about anything you ask for, it will be done for you by my Father in heaven. 'For where two or three come together in my name, there am I with them.'[11] So we can all three ask for the Lord's help now and know He is hearing us and will answer us." And that is what we did. Praying together at this moment for God's help for us and for everyone else made a big impact on both my sister and me. I remember thinking, "It's alright now; God is in charge!" and feeling quite light-hearted and wonderfully peaceful!

By now the dear cook and his wife were in deep distress, weeping and fearful, and the kebun (the gardener) was also in a great state, ringing his hands and wailing, "Susah! Susah!"[12]

I recall us all helping Eileen load her car, but what one took as normal in this extraordinary moment was a large cot mattress being tied to the roof of this tiny Austin 7. (Afterwards I discovered this was done to prevent any bullets entering through the roof!)

Mother took the little suitcase, and my father's Burberry raincoat which was hanging on the back of the door and, impulsively, also decided to bring her very best hat. Eileen took the three of us to the hotel at Tanah Rata, before returning to the Bank Bungalows to collect the others for their long drive to Kuala Lumpur. Somehow Eileen (at the steering wheel), her two sons and Kathleen with her two children were all squeezed into the miniature car. There was no room for their amah or their little dog, so she and the spaniel had to

---

[11] See Matthew 18:19-20
[12] 'Susah' means 'trouble'

be left behind. In tears they drove bravely off realising that they could meet the Japanese Army anywhere en route.[13]

We found it was eerily quiet at the hotel; there was no one about at all, just silence, apart from the sound of a few doors swinging on their hinges – all very strange indeed! There was no traffic, no movement anywhere; it seemed that everyone on the Hill had fled.

Lindsey and I played with an attractive stuffed real tiger in the hallway, enjoying this new game; it was a sort of normal thing to do! Suddenly, a voice was heard, and startled we all turned to find a kind Chinese man, probably a member of staff, asking what was happening and why we were there. Mother explained our circumstances and he, most thoughtfully, suggested making us some sandwiches! They were made from white bread and were delicious. We realised we were hungry and were all very grateful! He told us that the entire Hill was drained of any form of transport with many hundreds of panicking local people pouring down that incredible road (hopefully to safety) on bullock carts, bicycles, on foot and by whatever means possible.[14]

Presently, still at the hotel, we thought we could hear the noise of a car engine away in the distance. As it was so completely quiet with no sign of life anywhere, the sound carried a long way, from much further up the Hill. Mother hurried us up to the side of the road, with the suitcase, Father's raincoat and her hat, where we waited hopefully. And then we saw the car coming! I distinctly remember it was a dark green Ford. The driver looked incredulous; he stopped and asked what on earth we were doing, and Mother rapidly explained the situation. He sprang out of the car and hastily removed much of his luggage to allow the three of us to get in. He told Mother that he had not been able to depart any earlier because he was

---

[13] We realised that they did manage to get to Kuala Lumpur, and then, presumably, to Singapore, as we know that eventually they each returned to England. It was sad how difficult it was to keep in touch with friends with all that happened in this awful war.

[14] I wonder now why he was still there and if he had any plans to get away himself. Many people went into hiding that day, including our Chinese cook and amah. Years later we saw these dear folk again. They had had a terrible time under the Japanese, who were completely ruthless, shooting everyone in sight – but thankfully they had survived. I did not dare ask about the dog…

suffering a malarial fever too badly to go immediately on receiving the phone-call ordering him to leave the Hill, and was now rushing to get to his Army Unit in Ipoh. He thought it would be best to take us to the station at Tapah, where he hoped we would be able to catch a train to the south. He was in a great hurry. The road was very twisty, and there was no time to take the corners gently. No one knew where the Japs were; they could appear on the road at any moment.

He must have been an excellent driver and managed to cope with those forty miles of continuous hairpin bends magnificently; it was like racing down a helter-skelter! However, I had just enjoyed those appetising sandwiches, and not being a very good traveller at the best of times I began to feel ill. There was no time to stop! Mother offered me her lovely hat (it was the only thing to use under those circumstances) but I felt really bad about having to throw away such a prized possession!

We arrived at Tapah Station and this wonderful man (an answer to our prayers?) left us there to dash away to his Army Unit. I have often wondered what happened to him.

We managed to get onto the station platform, pushed to the edge because it was crowded – crowded with the people who had left Cameron Highlands so early that morning! Their luggage was piled up in heaps, and they were still waiting wearily in the tropical heat for a train which never seemed to come! Then, just as we had arrived, a train was heard coming, steaming and snorting, into the station. I had never seen a train like this one before because I noticed as it passed slowly by that there were dozens of little round holes on the sides of the wooden carriages as well as much obvious damage, and this fascinated me. Hissing noisily, the train gradually came to a standstill.

Pandemonium broke out. Everyone tried to rush on board at once with their baggage; the train was already overcrowded. Noise! Confusion! A window opened right in front of where we were standing, and before we knew quite what was happening, my sister and I were hauled aboard through the window by the strong arms belonging to some nuns! Their voices shouted in unison, "We must have the children's mother!" and Mother was swiftly pulled in through the door.

It's alright now – God is in charge!

At the same moment another voice was heard above all the commotion calling for "Mrs Lee!" Lee is quite a common Chinese name in Malaya so Mother did not respond straightaway, but there was an Indian man standing outside the carriage saying, "You are Mrs Lee, aren't you? I'd like to tell you that your husband was very, very good to me at one time!" Mother was a bit startled, but pleased to hear this and most surprised too when he handed her the huge basket of tropical fruit he was carrying! He explained, above the din and chaos all around, that he had just seen her arrive at the station and recognized her as the wife of a banker who had been so helpful to him, and that he would like her to accept the fruit he had quickly bought for her. Mother felt overwhelmed and very grateful too! Afterwards Mother wondered if this was an angelic visitation – the timing was so perfect and he vanished so quickly. This was an encouraging thought at such a tense moment!

She had the real pleasure of sharing this magnificent gift of fruit with everyone in the third class carriage we found ourselves in! Luscious rambutans, mangoes, mangosteens, bananas and more were all gratefully enjoyed, and as I had lost my sandwiches earlier, I was very glad too! We then heard that the nuns had had nothing to eat since leaving Penang and had had a horrific time, being machine-gunned by the Japanese Army on the way. But all this while, as we were settling thankfully into the carriage, the people from the Cameron Highlands were in anguish; they had just been warned to take only one suitcase each as otherwise there would be no room for all of them and their luggage, so they were having the awful problem of trying to decide what they could bring with them, if anything. This was an extremely fraught time for so many. It was actually easiest for us to have only our one small suitcase and father's raincoat! Eventually, the train started off for Kuala Lumpur with, hopefully, everybody on board, but there were a great many possessions left behind on the platform.

I remember feeling bewildered and utterly tired. Mother arranged Father's raincoat lovingly for me, and resting on the slats of the hard wooden seat seemed actually very comfortable! I slept while the nuns told their story and also rescued my poor sister from something that had got painfully into her eye. She remembers that very well as they were so kind to her. Just as we were about to arrive in Kuala Lumpur the nuns pointed out a small tree by the railway line that had beautiful little glowing lights all over it; it was truly a marvellous sight and has always been a lovely memory, particularly at that moment. Later we realised that the little tree was covered with a mass of fireflies.

By the time we actually got into the station at Kuala Lumpur, Japanese planes were bombing the town. Their army had not yet reached Kuala Lumpur, but their bombers were being deployed to all the main towns. Everybody was ordered to disembark from the train. Mother, placing our little suitcase carefully under a dim 'Exit' light, told the two of us to sit on it and that we were not to move. We sat wearily, back to back, carefully watching Mother all the time.

The old wooden railway carriage we photographed on Ipoh Station in 1993!

Mother joined the queue to try to buy tickets to continue our journey to Singapore, keeping a close eye on us through the crush of so many people. Suddenly, she heard her name being called – "Sheila, what are you doing here?" – and turning round she saw the local manager of the Hong Kong and Shanghai Bank beside her! He had heard about the train arriving in Kuala Lumpur and the influx of people and had come to see if he could help. It was wonderful that he saw her amongst the milling crowds and all the confusion! He immediately offered us accommodation, and before we knew what was happening we were whisked off to his lovely house. Several other rescued families were there already. Here I remember so well the care we were given, the relief of being with a kind amah who understood what was needed and what to do, and how the cook presented us with the most delicious scrambled egg I thought I had ever tasted!

The next few days were a nightmare! Mother tried persistently to get a train to Singapore, but with all the bombing and the whole chaotic situation there were hardly any trains available; they were needed to transport the Allied Troops. Everything was seriously disrupted. We both felt perfectly safe and secure with Mother, who continued to have a strong, serene faith, but when we were in other people's care, we picked up their understandable tensions and fear. Lindsey and I joined other children, including the Rix boys, at the Swimming Club, where some adults were helping by watching the children while their mothers were frantically busy. Sometimes we had to crawl under tables when Kuala Lumpur was being bombed, and suddenly the whole of our world seemed unfamiliar and crazy!

Despite that, I do recall one lovely moment of peace when Lindsey and I were playing at the bottom of the blue-carpeted stairs in the manager's house. I found myself saying over and over again the beautiful word 'beloved'; it was a new word to me and somehow gave me deep joy.[15]

I do not know how long we waited for a train – perhaps three days – but eventually there was one, and soon we were on our way overnight to Singapore and Father. Surely God had answered our prayers when we needed Him so much!

---

[15] Several years later I stayed again in this house with my fiancé, and this memory came back vividly!

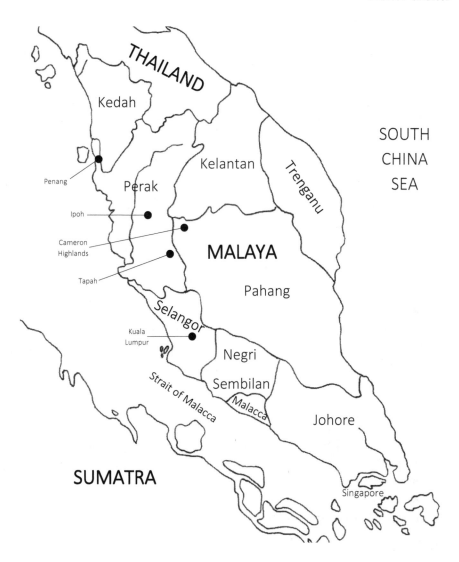

CHAPTER SEVEN

Mother's Dilemma

*P*art of Father's work at that time included arranging for the safe passage of many wives and children of the Hong Kong and Shanghai Bank from Singapore; it was hard on him that his own family were still upcountry. He was becoming increasingly concerned about their whereabouts and safety. At last, having heard from the manager of the bank in Kuala Lumpur that they were actually on their way to Singapore, he went to the station hopefully. There had been great problems about trains moving at all in the first chaotic days of the Japanese invasion of Malaya.

He waited wearily, having worked extremely hard in the bank during the day and then having been on duty with the Straits Settlement Volunteers at night. The house that his family would be moving into was brand new and not quite completed, but as the accommodation in Singapore was becoming acute with so many people coming from the north travelling to Singapore by whatever means possible, trusting that this would be a safe haven, it was best that Sheila and their girls should move in there at once. However, was Singapore really impregnable? He had serious doubts. He waited anxiously, uncertain about the future and what the best plans would be for his wife and seven-year-old daughters. He waited conscious of a great responsibility for his family, for the bank and for his unit of volunteers. He felt dizzy in the rising heat of the morning, but there was no time to think any more – the train was arriving and he greeted it with huge relief, sweeping his family first into his arms and then, with his raincoat and their one small suitcase, into the car, whisking them off to the new house, driving some way along the busy roads. He explained he would have to leave them to return quickly to his office; my parents had much to discuss as they sat together in the front seats.

I 'switched off' while they talked and thought how I liked to know where he worked; this would be the same office I remembered visiting with great awe on an earlier occasion. It was situated on the harbour front at Collier Quay and seemed huge. There were so many people sitting at their desks with a cacophony of noise from the clacking of typewriters, telephones ringing insistently, overhead fans, and much 'business talk', which was quite unintelligible to me. I had asked Father what everyone was doing, and lifting me up to sit on a high counter, he explained that there were many letters to be written, then that there were replies to these letters, and possibly more letters had to be typed in reply to those. There would also be phone calls to be made for all sorts of situations. People were discussing money matters and making decisions. Sums of money had to be carefully added up, often in long columns, and done absolutely correctly. I found these explanations were still totally mysterious. I quickly realised that I just wouldn't know how to begin to work in such a confusing place, nor would I ever want to; however, that was where Father had to go on our first morning back in Singapore, and I could easily visualise him there in that busy, noisy office with all those men concentrating so intensely on their work. I enjoyed thinking of him going to that enormous bank building near Keppel Harbour because the harbour was an endless delight to me. I loved the liveliness of all the ceaseless activity taking place – the ships of so many sorts and sizes; the industrious launches speeding between them with white foam streaking from their bows and sterns, ruffling up the smooth water into interesting waves and patterns; tugs fussing round some large liner, manoeuvring it into just the right position at the dockside; and colourful little sampans with Chinese people selling their wares.

I liked the sounds of the hooting and blowing of ships sirens, and calls of the boatmen. I enjoyed the smells of tar and ropes and even the coaling (or the loading of coal, a very messy, dusty work) for the larger ships, and always loved the salty smell of the sea. There were some strange unpleasant odours too, possibly drains or even sewage, but this was all part of the scene and seemed quite natural. Occasionally we might be there at the right time to watch the flying-boats arriving with the mail, swishing into the harbour, raising lovely curtains of spray on either side and then gliding to a halt. These would be met immediately by efficient launches taking the mailbags rapidly to the quayside. Perhaps there would be a letter for us amongst all the mail, and surely a great deal for Father's office.

My reverie ceased abruptly when we arrived at our house – and found it was so new that it smelled of wet concrete and that there was rubble lying about. It was one of a number of new ones being built in a Hong Kong and Shanghai Bank compound. It was furnished very sparsely with the bare necessities. Some iron bedsteads had been brought in. However, as the kitchen was not yet completed, there was a useful canteen nearby for meals. It was not easy to move into a not-quite-finished house, but Mother, as usual, made the best of the situation and cheerfully settled us in. She unpacked our small cane suitcase, looking ruefully at the few possessions she had managed to take before we fled from the Cameron Highlands. Thankfully, amongst other items, she had rescued her precious 'Daily Light', the devotional book with daily readings from the Bible which she had used for many years. She gave it a little pat with a grateful sigh, placing it carefully on a table and realising how sorry she would have been had this treasure been left behind. She also found her dressing-table-set that my father had given her as a wedding present and that she used every day – another loved treasure. There were trunks and storage boxes to be unpacked and much to sort out. She expected that Father would return in the evening when they would discuss what the priorities would have to be and would do some necessary shopping. Naturally he had the car; there was no other transport for the family at that time.

I remember that there was a friendly lady next door to us who invited Lindsey and me, with several other children too, into her house to visit her. Her house must have been completed, I suppose, for she had pictures on her walls, one of which was of Jesus with a group of children who were all of different nationalities. She told us about Jesus and His love for children and quietly said that He loved each of us too. I found this very reassuring and comforting to think about again at another bewildering time. I was not well, and these confusing days merged rather hazily as far as I was concerned, but the lady and her picture remain as an inspiring memory.

I recall asking if I could play with Mother's beautiful hairbrush and mirror set, and she lovingly let me, saying, "Yes, you may look at them, but you know that I really treasure these things, so you will be very careful, won't you? As you aren't very well, why not rest quietly on the bed and play gently with them there." I assured her that I would be very careful and happily carried each item to the bed and sat there gazing at the pretty enamel and silver work. Each brush or mirror of this charming set was edged in silver and backed with enamel in a lovely golden yellow, making me think of sunshine. I carefully turned the hairbrush over and enjoyed seeing how the pattern of the enamel cleverly radiated out from the centre. The clothes brush and comb were basically similar and so attractive. Then I looked at the mirror, and here, again, although the shape was rather like the hairbrush, it also had the unique pattern lines. I loved it all. I turned the mirror over and pulled a face at my reflection. I had always wished that I had had long fair hair and there was still only my short dark hair, but today I would just pretend it was the blond hair that I fancied so much, falling down my back in a cascade of curls. I picked up the hairbrush and with long careful sweeps of my arm I brushed my imaginary locks contentedly. The time passed peacefully, and some while later I returned all these treasures to the dressing-table, taking great care and somehow feeling very privileged to have been allowed to handle them.

Mother waited for Father all that evening, then all the following day and into the next one too, with growing disquiet. The phone had not yet been installed, but I think our kind neighbour must have let us use hers. No one from the bank knew where he was; he had not been seen at all. This was cause for even more concern. She wondered if perhaps he had been called away unexpectedly for some training.

Mother met some of the other wives already settled in their new houses on the compound, telling them about our flight from the north and how steadily the Japanese Army was approaching. She tried to warn them of imminent disaster but they refused to listen to her, angrily accusing her of worrying them because Singapore was surely invincible, everyone knew that, so what was she doing lowering their morale in this dangerous way? These people were probably amongst those whom Father was urging to leave Singapore while it was still possible.

Then, suddenly, Father appeared, looking dreadfully ill and very worried. He had collapsed unconscious on the way to the office that first morning. Some passer-by had helped to get him promptly into hospital where he was tended until he regained consciousness, but with a high fever he was delirious for a while. No one there knew who he was. He was desperate to return to his stranded family, and 'escaping' from the hospital as soon as he possibly could, he first managed to return to the bank, caught up on the latest situation there and then hurried back to us.

Mother was shocked by his appearance. He was really ill but had very urgent news for us. My parents retreated to their bedroom and were in deep conversation for some while. Years later Mother told me what happened at this crucial time. They sat together by the window of the room and Father said that he had just heard of a ship, a small Canadian Lake Steamer, a cargo ship, where the six officers on board were offering their cabins for the use of women and children fleeing from Malaya. The ship was to sail that night.

Mother looked at him with huge concern. "Darling, you are too ill. I simply will not hear of leaving you, especially at this time."

"But," his reply was firm and sad, "this is such an opportunity; it may not happen again. You must go, this very evening, and take the children to a safe country, possibly South Africa, and accept this magnificent offer."

Mother was equally adamant. "No, I will stay and look after you."

What a dilemma!

They argued passionately. Just then her eye was caught by the movement of the pages of her little 'Daily Light' on the table beside them; the pages were gently turning and came to a stop. Her eye fell on a sentence from the book of the prophet Micah which said, "Arise ye, and depart; for this is not your rest; because it is polluted, it shall destroy you even with a sore destruction." [16] She gazed with wonder at this verse. Was the page open just because a little breeze came in at the open window at that exact moment? She felt deep within herself

---

[16] Micah 2:10, Authorized Version, from the reading for 26th July.

that this was surely a word from the Lord. If it really was that, who was she to defy his warning?

She pointed quietly to the page, and Father, seeing those significant words, had no further need to persuade her.

Together they gathered a few things – amongst these were some clothes, a tiny Persian floor rug, a favourite picture, the 'Daily Light', and the treasured hairbrush set from Father – and they swiftly packed a few suitcases. They called Lindsey and me, telling us that we were going to find the ship that would take us on the next part of our journey. By now we were so used to travelling with all the surprising things that seemed to be constantly happening that we confidently set off with our two parents and made our way to Singapore harbour.

I remember that we stopped at a large shop en route. There were Christmas decorations and exciting things to see, and I wanted to remind my parents that it would be a good idea to do some Christmas shopping. Sensing that they had far more important things on their minds, I reluctantly refrained from making this suggestion, but while they were busy with their vital shopping, I looked wistfully at a wonderful display of possible presents, all kinds of tempting toys and little cuddly creatures – available yet so completely out of reach!

We left the shop, and I recall a great sense of regret and disappointment; however, it was time to take a small launch out to our ship, always an exciting thing to do. The short dusk of the tropics was almost over as we approached. We all climbed the swaying gangway onto the deck and were warmly greeted by smiling men in their white uniforms.

The ship astonished me. I was used to large passenger liners, and this seemed such a tiny ship; everything was on a very small scale which was intriguing. It was a cargo ship with accommodation only for the crew. We were shown the officers' cabins. I think there were six of these, three on either side of the ship with a narrow corridor serving each side and meeting at right angles fore and aft.

There were interior bathrooms off these corridors. The cabins had two bunks with a narrow aisle between them and just a small amount of storage space, and they each had one porthole. I call to mind that everything was very basic but so clean and well polished. As I still wasn't very well, I was to share a cabin with Mother, on the starboard side of the ship, and a bunk was found for my sister on the port side, sharing a cabin with a lady who was expecting her first baby. Mercifully my sister and I were not aware of the critical times we were in or of the impending bombing of Singapore, and our parents settled us down into our usual bedtime routine. Presently I crept out of bed and peeped out to see what was happening. I saw my parents in each other's arms on the deck, quietly talking and perhaps praying; they stayed like that for what seemed a very long time. They were both in great distress. I realised something of their intense sorrow, of their profound love for one another, and to some degree something of the agony of parting from each other. They were saying goodbye. It was a most poignant moment which I believe went very deep into my subconscious. All the while, as my parents were clasped together in each other's arms, they were silhouetted against enormously high flames and spectacular 'fireworks' that seemed to fill the sky. [17]

I do not remember Father saying goodbye to me. I think he tried, perhaps, to make it uneventful when he said goodnight. We were so used to his coming and going that I imagine he would try to make it seem quite ordinary, but I also think he would have to conceal his emotions as I know he was very sad. What could he say, not knowing when any of us would ever see each other again, perhaps even *if* ever?

When I woke the following morning we were well out to sea. My dear father and Singapore, with its troubles, seemed far behind us, but there was still more to come in the long voyage and dangerous seas before us.

---

[17] The huge petrol storage tanks on an island off Singapore were on fire; they had been set alight by the British as a precaution against a possible Japanese invasion. There was an air raid taking place too, with loud sound effects, but I did not understand the significance then.

CHAPTER EIGHT

SS Colborne

*T*he 'SS Colborne' was a Canadian Lakes steamer of some six thousand tons. She was a cargo ship, and the story goes that the captain, a young man who had succeeded his father as the owner, had responded to a dare to sail round the world; to finance the voyage; cargoes were bought and sold en route! This makes an intriguing yarn, but we have no way to verify it. We do know, however, that she was the last ship to pick up a cargo of rubber from Malaya before the Japanese invasion.

She was docked in Penang when the Japanese bombed the town and harbour so disastrously on 11th December, 1941. I was delighted when I found that two of the officers on board had each been awarded the MBE for firing at the Japanese aircraft responsible!

I believe the captain and his six officers, having seen the devastating effects of the Japanese unexpected bombing of Penang, generously decided on offering to give up their cabins to women and children to help them flee from the Japanese, whom of course they had just seen in action and had understood the consequences of the invasion. They then sailed south to Singapore and anchored in Keppel Harbour.

In the records seen at the Maritime Museum at Greenwich it was noted that the Colborne spent about a week in Singapore, from 14th to 22nd December; was this to repair the shrapnel damage from the bombing, I wonder?

Then, having got their grateful passengers carefully on board ship, they steamed out to sea in the dark night hours, safely away from the air attack on Singapore. The passengers included my mother, Lindsey and me; my father remained in Singapore working in the Hong Kong and Shanghai Bank and was a member of the Straits Settlement Volunteer Forces.

Being a freight steamer, the accommodation was above decks at one end, with the holds taking up the remainder of the ship. Besides the cabins we were given, we also had the use of the small saloon with space for a table for meals. There were several children with their mothers, of course, and then there was one man. I do not know why he was on board, but he was very nervous, more so than anyone else. Later, we wondered if he was suffering from some post-traumatic stress? I recall him scolding my sister and me when we were laughing happily about something, demanding angrily, "How can you two children laugh when we are all in such serious trouble, stop it at once!"

We were strictly instructed to have our life jackets nearby at all times and at night to have clothes beside us to wear in case there was an emergency. No lights whatsoever were permitted after dusk, not even the glow from a lighted cigarette, and constantly there was the reminder to be very careful with the use of fresh water. All this added to the tension that undoubtedly was on board. Though the captain and his men were always kind to us all, we instinctively recognized their authority and respected their orders.

The Indian Ocean was teeming with enemy shipping, both Japanese and German, and it was a perilous place to be at that time. The Colborne had to continually take evasive action, and zigzagged all the way as we were not sailing in convoy. This seemed a familiar way to sail the seas to me; I remembered on the two previous voyages our ships had taken the same strange course, so I thought that perhaps 'these days' that was the real way to sail, tacking as if in a yacht! There were dangers from U-boats and other German or Japanese vessels all the time, and precautions were carried out continually.

I particularly remember one of the young officers in his attractive white uniform. The sun was shining on him, he looked so tanned and I thought he looked dashingly handsome. He was standing by the gun which was mounted firmly on the after deck near the stern of the ship, with one foot placed on its support. He told us with great pride,

"This gun is the only one that was fired in defence of Penang!" I gazed at it with suitable awe. I knew about guns; had not much bigger guns than this been installed pointing out to sea by our hotel in Singapore? I reminisced how my sister and I had enjoyed playing in the gorgeous heaps of sand that had presumably been used for the cementing in of the huge gun. So this little gun had actually been fired against the enemy? I did not really understand that bit but it sounded very important, and I also touched the gun with a feeling of pride and almost affection!

Lindsey reminded me how the children were allowed to throw a disk into the sea which was then fired on with this gun to make a smoke screen – this 'famous' gun which was used against bears in Canada!

A few days into the voyage and it was Christmas Day. Lindsey and I had no presents; they had been overlooked after all in our rush to get away from Singapore! The other mothers had prepared for Christmas, remembering such an important event in good time, it seemed, and all the children had the excitement of opening their gifts except for the two of us. One mother firmly forbade her son to share his chocolates with us as we would have nothing with which to reciprocate. The kind officers realised our plight, and between them they found each of us a little present which we treasured for years. I do not recall what my sister's gift was, but I was thrilled with a charming little eggcup.

One day my sister played with the electric plug by her bunk and received quite a serious shock. Her whole hand was blackened with soot, and terrified she fled to our mother. She needed much comforting. We were both given a severe warning to never, never play with electrical things; it was a lesson that neither of us would ever forget. As a consequence of this near disaster Mother decided it was time for us to swap cabins so it became my turn to share with the pregnant lady, who by now Mother had particularly befriended.

I found this lady to be sweet and gentle but extremely shy. It must have been heartbreaking for to leave her husband and to face an unknown future with a new baby, and I felt very sorry for her. She used to lie quietly on her bunk for long periods, and though she was thrilled about her coming baby, I think she wept at times.

It's alright now – God is in charge!

Although life on board ship settled into some routine, there was much tension with tangible fear, and this was conveyed to all of us children; however, the ship's crew tried to amuse us in many ways, allowing us to 'help' in various little chores. I remember that one never knew what would happen next, and how much safer we felt when with Mother. Amongst other things, she always made our bath times such fun; there was no shortage of sea water so we could have lovely deep, splashy baths. Occasionally it would come with some phosphorescence which sparkled delightfully; we all enjoyed this tremendously. Looking back now, I wonder if there was otherwise very little fun and laughter on board this ship?

One night, in the cabin I shared with the lady, with all the fear of so much danger around us, I had a dream which was wonderful to me. I dreamt that I was in a beautiful wood walking with Jesus. I just knew it was *Him*. He was holding my right hand, and I was skipping along to his more measured stride. He was tall, strong and kind, caring and understanding. It all seemed perfectly normal and natural, and as we walked together, with me doing a little skip every now and again, I knew the deepest sense of security and assurance that one could possibly imagine, and that all was well. We then came out of the lovely wood into a sort of barren place where there was a steep, very high, red laterite cliff which looked forbidding and impossible to climb. I recall surveying this, not understanding what it meant, but still feeling wonderfully safe. We looked at each other, and in silent agreement we returned to the peaceful wood with the birds singing and sunlight reaching through the trees, lighting up fresh green leaves, and walked alongside a bubbling stream with such clear water that we could even see everything on the little riverbed – the colourful pebbles and then the plants swaying in the water, being stretched out in the flowing movement. I loved the way sunlight sparkled on the little wavelets and the sheer loveliness of the whole scene. But what struck me most of all, as my hand was so gently yet firmly held, was the feeling of complete security, of being totally understood, and I knew that I was incredibly loved, and accepted just as I was, a rather fearful little girl. It was an amazing dream, and I woke feeling utterly secure and peaceful. I knew then that there was nothing to fear. Jesus was with me, he held my hand, he was my friend and I loved him; he loved and cared for me, and if that was so for me, it was true for every one of us!

This was a life-changing experience and has stayed with me ever since; there have been many, many times when I've been afraid and recalled the dream and remembered the great assurance of my hand securely held in Jesus'! I just need to remember to remember! I am not sure if I could talk about this dream properly to my mother, but she told me much later that I became much more serene and confident, and she realised something must have happened to me. As her own deep faith was so based on Jesus Christ, she could understand.

In due course we arrived at Colombo, Ceylon, as it was known in those days. How busy the harbour was, what activity! It was all so delightfully familiar with its sounds, sights and smells, and yet so different with dark-skinned people speaking another interesting language to my ears. This harbour was seething with ships and people; the whole place seemed alive and vibrant! We were encouraged to disembark while our ship was being refuelled with coal as there would be a great deal of dust about. The ship also took on much-needed supplies and water.

Mother swept us off to shop for a belated Christmas present; it was so exciting to go into a large and colourful shop and find the place full of marvellous games and toys! What choices there were before us! How hard it was to know what we would really like the best; it was such an important decision to make! We each took a long time looking, which was part of the fun, and in the end I chose a game. This was in an attractive box with a perforated board into which were placed little hyacinth-like flowers that could be arranged into pretty patterns. I was enchanted with this and enjoyed playing with this creative toy for a long time to come. Lindsey found some building blocks and was also very pleased with her interesting present.

Mother planned to take us out to the Galle-face Hotel at Mount Lavinia. This seemed a very special place and all the more so when Mother told us she had come to this hotel when she about eight years old too, on her way back to England from Japan with her parents. I looked up at the high ceilings and architecture of this magnificent building with even greater awe, exclaiming, "Then this must be a very, very old building!" I knew it must surely be extremely ancient if it was in existence such a long time ago, when my mother was a child, and was puzzled then that she was obviously very amused by my comments.

After a short while in port, our ship was ready to sail again, and we steamed quietly out of Colombo docks; this time the Colborne was en route for South Africa and ultimately Lake Ontario, Canada. Our call at Ceylon was a welcome respite, but we were soon back in the Indian Ocean where enemy shipping still lurked menacingly.

We steamed steadily along, the engines throbbing, and the sea parting on either side of the bows, turning over gracefully in curling waves. We would often see flying fish, and occasionally porpoises would accompany us, diving in and out of the sea, playing alongside the ship and delighting us all. And behind the ship the foaming wake followed us all the way; looking further behind we could see where the ship made its zigzag turns and where, in the distance, the white wake gently petered out. I always loved the sea – the sparkles and little rainbows that appeared in the bow waves, the constantly changing shapes and patterns of the lively ocean. I loved the different shades of blue, from deep indigo to pale translucent turquoises and greens. Thankfully, I did not realise what foes may have been below just out of sight because – alas, distressingly – much later we discovered that several other ships with people (including children) on board had suffered terrible fates from enemy submarines and action.

It was exciting to sail by the Seychelles and other islands; we could see enchanting places. Decades later my sister and her husband would return on holiday to these lovely islands to explore them properly. But in spite of idyllic-looking surroundings we were always in danger and very short of water. We still had to be extremely careful about the use of fresh water, showing no lights whatever, and having lifebelts constantly at hand, the captain being responsible for taking all possible precautions for our safety.

One day there was a terrifying moment. A British warship (perhaps a cruiser), which looked enormous to us, seemed to suddenly loom up. It made signals to our lake-steamer, and for some reason our captain must have raised the wrong flag in return. The warship slowly turned and aimed every one of its magnificent looking guns straight down at our ship, a truly awesome sight –

74

unforgettable! There was an urgent call for all the passengers to come out onto the deck. I believe this was to show that our ship was carrying women and children. The captain must then have made the correct signal – such relief all round! The Royal Naval vessel stopped being so bristly and made a dignified departure; it had serious business to do. But, much to the captain's dismay, it did not respond to his request for fresh water; this was ignored, and the mighty ship continued on its way, disappearing rapidly below the far distant horizon.

As we approached Durban, there was another scary event when several planes flew low over our ship; were they inspecting us suspiciously? However, we sailed on, rounding the southern-most tip of South Africa where the two oceans meet, and eventually, on 21st January, arriving at the Cape, docking in Cape Town with the familiar sight of Table Mountain in the background.

After a delay, for some reasons of red-tape, we were able to disembark here. Mother made this decision thinking that, having lived there before, we would feel more at home in South Africa; Canada was totally unfamiliar to her. Soon the SS Colborne was back at sea with her wonderful captain and officers and all the crew who had been so magnificently generous to us fugitives, a gesture we would always remember with deep thankfulness! This time she sailed via the Atlantic Ocean en route for home in Canada. From a letter sent by the pregnant lady, now a new mother, telling us of the birth of her son, we knew that the Colborne had arrived safely![18]

We had come a long way shielded from harm, all the way from the Cameron Highlands, unscathed by enemy action. We were saved from horrors in Malaya, as yet unknown to us at that time. Although, naturally, Mother had great anguish over my father and their parting, she realised much of the significance of our escape and was immeasurably grateful to God.

Another life was soon to begin, this time as refugees, and we were presently to discover the kindness and hospitality of the South Africans in a new way. However, Father was about to find out that his life was also to change dramatically under the regime of the Japanese; here there would be no kind hospitality whatsoever!

---

[18] My husband and I also discovered this in our visit to the Maritime Museum in London, as well as a few other dates of this voyage.

It's alright now – God is in charge!

SS Colborne

SS Colborne sailed from Penang on 12th December, 1941 and arrived in Singapore on 14th December, 1941. She then departed from Keppel Harbour, Singapore, on 22nd December, 1941 and arrived at Cape Town, via Colombo, on 21st January, 1942.

SS Colborne was built in 1921 in Vancouver by Wallace SB&DD Co. Ltd, owned by Canadian Skirmisher Ltd and was managed by Canadian National Steamships Co. Ltd. Her gross tonnage was 6,230. She may have been scrapped by 1948.

The two officers from the CN Steamship Colborne who received MBEs for firing the gun at the Japanese bombers in the air attack over Penang were named Douglas Lealand Creaser MBE (Second Officer) and Douglas Gordon Dauphine MBE (Third Officer), both from Nova Scotia. The MBEs were awarded to them in June 1945.

The small vessels loading the ship with rubber in Penang Harbour were sunk in the Japanese air-raid attack, but while the Colborne suffered some damage (about fifty holes in the hull) and Hold No 3 started to fill with water, she was still able to sail to Singapore with her valuable cargo of rubber.

CHAPTER NINE

The Cape and Lah-di-dah

We arrived at South Africa on 21st January (1942) after our voyage from Malaya, and it was wonderful to be back in this lovely part of the world. The Cape itself is a very beautiful place with so much variation in its spectacular scenery from the dramatic mountains to the sea coasts and beaches; some of the latter have huge rollers roaring in that are famous for good surfing. Having rounded the Cape of Good Hope, we steamed at last into Cape Town harbour. Here Table Mountain towers protectively over the town and its busy dockyards; it seemed dear and familiar.

With some kind South African friends from Muizemberg being able to vouchsafe for us, we disembarked, collecting our small amount of luggage, and proceeded through the customs control. It was somewhere here that I remember us being called "refugees" for the first time, and even though I did know what that meant, I could tell that Mother reacted with shocked surprise; perhaps this was a new idea to her too.

Arrangements were made for us to go the excellent YWCA hostel in Muizemberg, The Towers, where we had stayed about eighteen months before, on our first arrival in South Africa. The manageress, Hilary Steynor, greeted us warmly and quickly made us feel at home. To our joy, Lindsey and I found that (for a reason I never discovered) she had kept our little dolls from the time we had stayed there again, just before our voyage to Singapore some six months earlier. Being reunited with my doll meant a great deal to me, and I crooned happily over her and took great care of her, vowing never to be parted again.

We stayed at this hostel for some time while Mother tried to make plans for our future. In those days many children were being evacuated away from the dangers of the German bombings and the Blitz, and there was no possibility of finding a ship to return to England. However, although we were always glad to be together, it was awful not having Father with us, and particularly hard for Mother.

There was a large building next door to The Towers, and one of my vivid memories was of a great many little boys and girls arriving there quite soon after we did but without either of their parents. They had just been evacuated from England, and my heart went out to them all. Not having either of their parents with them was distressing to me; I empathized strongly and grieved for each one of them, knowing a little of how I would feel in their place. I longed to be able to comfort them, as it was obvious that these young children were homesick and traumatized. In the end I also needed much consoling and then was most relieved to know that each one of them was to go to a lovely home with people who wanted to take care of them at this time. Later I was also very glad to hear that the children would all be returning to their own families as soon as the War was over.

Mother had arranged for a young teenager to help take care of Lindsey and me for a while; her name was Lois, and we soon became friends. She would take us for walks and down to the beach, pausing at a large open space if there was a parade, which occasionally took place. How I loved these! The bands always delighted me, and I greatly admired the soldiers in their smart uniforms, marching in time to the music. The War was far away and we only saw these glamorous parts, so at this stage it was all most interesting and safe.

However, there was a day when Lois came in weeping, and she told Mother something that she was obviously most shocked and distressed about. I saw Mother gently trying to comfort her, but it wasn't until our bath-time that Lois told us through renewed tears what had upset her so much. She had heard of a ship, full of evacuee children coming from England to the safety of South Africa, which had been sunk by the Germans. I was utterly appalled. I remembered clearly what it was to be on a ship and could visualise all too well what it must have been like for a ship to be sunk. I could imagine the terror of the children, especially as they were without their mothers, and was absolutely devastated by this awful story. I joined Lois in her tears and have never forgotten this horrific event. For years I could not bear to think of sinking ships, and sometimes in a bath or swimming pool the memory would come back and I'd imagine how a ship could sink, with the utmost dread. Even now, I do not like looking at submerged wrecks, and although I realise why this is, I still feel a real horror.

Once I had a nightmare about being bombed and was terrified and upset. Mother came to me in the night and, putting her arms around me, asked lovingly what the trouble was. I sobbed, "There was a bomb – and it was so frightening!"

Mother tried to console me. "That was an abominable dream!" she said and reminded me of the wonderful dream I had had about Jesus and how safe I had felt with him. That remembrance soon made all the difference, and presently she had me laughing in trying to repeat after her the word 'abominable' – 'a bomb in a bull'! The merriment released the fear, and soon I was peacefully asleep again.

Mother had had a lovely friend when we lived in St James's Bay the year before, a Mrs McNab. She was my sister's godmother's godmother! They renewed their friendship and Mrs McNab was once again very kind to us. She was a loving support to Mother who certainly needed this very much at that time. When she realised Mother had not got a Bible with her any more, just her precious little book 'Daily Light' with its portions of Scriptures set for every day, Mrs McNab gave her a very nice leather-bound Bible. This had been presented to her on retirement from some women's organization, and it immediately became one of Mother's treasures.[19]

---

[19] In 1997, when Hugh and I returned to South Africa on holiday, we visited the church that Mrs McNab used to attend at Kenilworth, Cape Town. I had brought the Bible that Mrs McNab had given Mother in order to give it to the church as an act of thanksgiving for the wonderful way God had cared for us all during our years of refugees and in memory of dear Mrs McNab. To our delight and astonishment two elderly sisters there said to us that they remembered Mrs McNab too, and what a loving person she was to them also. They used to live quite near to her. It was amazing that we were able to join in with our own heartfelt thanks to the Lord at the church's very special Thanksgiving Service.

It's alright now – God is in charge!

Then 15th February, 1942 dawned with the terrible news of the fall of Singapore, and Miss Steynor, who had heard the news earlier, arranged the chairs at our breakfast table so that only Mother's back would be visible to the rest of the guests staying at the hostel. She knew that she would be dreadfully distressed on hearing the usual morning news broadcast and wanted to protect her as much as possible from everyone's stares. Mother remembers being very grateful indeed for that thoughtful kindness.

Soon afterwards Mother received a letter from Father; it was written just before Singapore fell. I am amazed at the way it reached us (there must have been a ship at just the right moment sailing from Singapore) and not only a letter but, to our great joy, parcels from Father for my sister and me as well. We opened these eagerly and were each excited to find our own beautiful sets of baskets. Lindsey's was purple and mine a deep bright red. Inside each of the largest baskets was another one and within that another until we found four lovely baskets of varying sizes. We piled these baskets up one above the other and took them rather precariously in our arms to show Miss Steynor, who duly admired them too. I still have three of my baskets, but the smallest one perished long ago, having served most usefully as a pencil box for many years.

It was incredibly special to have these baskets from Father, and I was absolutely thrilled with this loving gesture. It was something that I often thought about in the years to come, reminding me of what Father was really like. We heard no more from him. We had just three P.O.W. postcards in the three-and-a-half years to follow... but that is another story.

A short while later it was our eighth birthday, and there was another lovely thing that Miss Steynor did which I always remember with pleasure. When Lindsey and I came to our breakfast table we found that both our chairs had been beautifully decorated with flowers. This was such a glorious surprise! There were flowers of all colours, shapes and sizes entwined over and around the backs of the chairs, looking spectacular, with a smiling Miss Steynor wishing us a Happy Birthday. I do not remember anything else about that birthday otherwise, but it is sheer delight to recall that stunning sight and to feel that someone cared that much about us.

While Mother was trying to decide what we should be doing in the future, she was asked to help with the local Girl Guides. Not being a very practical person, I don't think she enjoyed this very much. I remember seeing her practising folding a man's shirt properly before she was to show the Guides what to do and wishing I could learn too. I thought that one day it would be so useful to know how to do this when Father was with us again, but she didn't teach us useful things like that; it just did not occur to her to do so!

We liked going to the little local church, and I particularly loved the hymn 'Onward Christian Soldiers' because I knew that Father was a soldier and I thought it had a great and rousing tune. In fact there were several meaningful hymns with lovely words, some of which, in the Sunday School, had actions which were fun to do. There must have been a really nice atmosphere and loving people that I remember it all so fondly.

After a while we moved on to a lovely place called Montagu; this was further east and situated in spectacular mountains in the "Little Karoo". There were marvellous hot springs there and a swimming pool. This was a touch of heaven to my sister and me, and we enjoyed a greater freedom. However, I remember that Mother, who was about forty and very beautiful, had an admirer whom we did not like. On one occasion when he called, my sister and I told him firmly that Mother was not in and so would not be able to see him. I don't think he ever came again, and I wonder if he realised our antagonism. When at last we confessed this to Mother I think she was mostly relieved, though just a little sorry not to have another friend.

Mother was continuing to make enquiries about the possibilities for our very uncertain future, and it must have been a very difficult time for her. We then stayed at a modest hotel near the sea at Gordon's Bay. Here Lindsey and I tried to learn to fish. We each found a long stick, and fastening a length of string to these we then attached safety pins as 'hooks' – and were delighted with our new 'fishing rods'! I think it was just as well that we didn't ever catch any fish because I wonder what we would have done, neither of us liking to touch such things and certainly not to kill them! Mother was actually quite discouraging – wisely, perhaps, as no doubt she would not have liked any success on our part at all!

It was on the beach at Gordon's Bay that she instilled into us one evening at dusk that we must be very careful of strangers, particularly if anyone appeared to be drunk. She pointed to a man who seemed to be walking most unsteadily and peculiarly towards us. This man really worried me though I did not understand what "being drunk" was; I only knew it must be a very dangerous condition and one definitely to be avoided!

It was here too that as a family of refugees we were each given some new clothes. We had very little with us, and while I thought these clothes (some skirts with cardigans to match) were wonderful and was ecstatic over them, Mother was strangely unhappy. I simply could not understand why this should be; the clothes were so pretty, I thought. Perhaps she was beginning to realise more and more about our new refugee status – I just don't know – but she was quite distressed and I did not know how to comfort her.

At about this time Lindsey and I had a marvellous invitation: would Mother allow us to visit a farmer and his wife, whom she had met at the Gordon's Bay hotel, to stay for a while at their farm? This was at Somerset East, a long train journey away. Mother agreed and we were very excited. The plan was that she would accompany us on the train to Somerset East and leave us there with this lovely couple for about ten days before returning to collect us again. Making sure that she would come back for us, we set off gaily on the night train. We had a compartment with several other people, and Lindsey and I had to share a bunk, with our heads at either end to give us a little more space. We were met by a pair of friendly South African farmers. I wish I could remember their names; we just knew them as 'Uncle' and 'Auntie' and grew very fond of them. They were so good to us and very kind, teaching us so much on our brief visit there. We were driven to their farmstead, and Mother saw where we were going before being taken back to the station to catch a train to return to the Cape area again.

The farm had the unusual name of 'Lah-di-dah' and was huge. The farmer and his wife told us that it was "approximately ten miles by ten miles" which was "one hundred square miles", and it did seem enormous to us as we were driven along the rough country roads.

It was mainly a sheep farm. We learnt how sheep were cared for as we were taken in the farm truck to inspect the various parts of the farm and saw how important it was for Uncle, as the farmer, to keep an eye on every part of the farm and to watch over all his stock.

The sheep were being sheared at this time, and we were allowed to watch every part of the intriguing process. I very much admired the skill and speed with which the sheep were sheared – it seemed so easily done – and then we saw how astonishingly different the sheep looked without their huge woolly coats. It was so interesting to hear what the next stage would be for the wool. Described simply for us, we were told that first this was bundled carefully but rapidly into a neat roll; it was then to be washed before being spun; and then, after spinning, it could be used for so many things, knitted into garments or turned into rugs and blankets. It was all most fascinating.

The farmhouse was a typical one-storey building and had the usual stoep[20]. This was the main place to be, where we would sit chatting with Auntie and Uncle and learning more about life on the farm. I loved the way they told us so much and how they were obviously keen that we should understand their way of life.

The two of us shared a bedroom and were told that we should have a rest each afternoon as it was quite hot then. We didn't like this much, and those were the times we felt rather homesick. The only other thing that made us slightly rebellious was the morning routine that seemed expected of us and which we never thought about with our mother. We were to go to the 'little house' every day after breakfast – "It is most important to have regular habits, and people's bowels should be opened every day," Auntie told us. I am not sure who was the most shocked, Auntie or us, by our lack of this good habit that clearly should have been instilled into us a long time before!

Soon it was Easter, and we had such a lovely surprise on Easter Sunday morning. Auntie had made each of our dolls some beautiful clothes, and we were over the moon about them. They were enchanting diminutive dresses, skilfully made to fit these precious 'babies' of ours, and I felt it was just wonderful that she cared enough to make them. In fact we were so well taken care of and so lovingly understood that the visit did much to help us at such a strange and bewildering time. Later Mother told us that this lovely couple wanted

---

[20] verandah

to adopt us – they really loved us – but naturally Mother wouldn't hear of it!

In the meanwhile Mother was still wondering about the best plan for our future. The news, when there was any, was very bad from the Far East, and she simply did not know what was happening to Father. This was a very sad time for her, and I know she was suffering deeply. The people round about her in Gordon's Bay were wonderfully good, and were really concerned about our situation. They tried to help her and were so kind, taking her to many beautiful places in that area. She particular remembers going to some vineyards and seeing some of the lovely buildings with Dutch gables and the wonderful gardens and farms, some of which were in the mountains with fantastic views. Years later, though, when she saw photographs of my visit to South Africa with Hugh, she told that she remembered vividly the grief she had felt at that sad time.

One day someone at the hotel told Mother excitedly that she had heard of a Christian community further east, beyond Somerset East, where there was an invitation for a Christian family of refugees to join them.

"You are a Christian, Sheila," she was told enthusiastically, "why not think about this idea? I believe it could be just the answer for you and your daughters." So Mother considered this amazing offer very prayerfully and decided it was the right solution to what was proving to be a very difficult situation.

She accepted the invitation with deep appreciation, and plans were made for the move to what was to be a wonderful home for a long time to come. Our little family was about to start a new life once again, and trustingly we put our lives into the capable hands of the Lord, knowing that he was guiding us and that he would surely continue to take good care of us all.

CHAPTER TEN

The Hope

*I*t was Mrs Mahon of 'The Hope' farm who had asked if there were any refugees who would like to stay at her home for the duration of the War. She specifically asked for a Christian family, explaining that she was part of a Christian community and felt that such a family would fit in happily.

So once again our family were on the move. We took the train from Cape Town and were advised to travel as far north as De Aar before changing trains for one which would get us to our destination, a little place called Mortimer. In fact the advice was not helpful as the route was unnecessarily long. The journey took three days where, if we had only realised this and taken the train via Port Elizabeth, it would have been considerably shorter. However, the long train journey was a very interesting experience and one which we always remembered.

The train was fairly comfortable. The three of us shared a compartment with seats that at night were intriguingly transformed into bunks. My sister and I had fun exploring the train and discovered that every carriage had two compartments with three bunk beds and that there were further eight compartments with six bunk beds each. Every compartment had a little washbasin and a pull-out table; there were toilets at either end of the carriages shared by everyone. A friendly African man walked the length of the train playing a four-note gong announcing when a meal was about to be served; these meals were a feature of the long days and beautifully produced.

It's alright now – God is in charge!

The very long train was pulled by two powerful engines, either both at the front or sometimes at each end, though very occasionally three engines were necessary. One had to be careful at any open window because of the smuts blowing back from the steam engines; these could be painful in an eye and were also very dirty. The scenery we passed through was magnificent and quite variable from flat veldt country (almost desert) to spectacular mountains. We would gaze out of the windows, fascinated by the wide empty expanse of this amazing country, or spellbound with the marvellous views of towering peaks and valleys of breathtaking beauty. Just occasionally we could see ostriches on the plains, and sometimes, as we pointed out to each other excitedly, baboons sitting on fences. There were only a few stops in the sparsely populated country, but the people who could come would be at these tiny stations, eager to sell their wares or to collect any mail and provisions – the train providing some sort of focal point and importance to their day.

Starting off again from a station was always interesting and usually very noisy with the guard blowing his whistle loudly and the engine responding slowly with a huge amount of effort – hooting and puffing hard, straining to get going again. There were times, mostly at night, when shunting took place, with the whole train and all its passengers being startled by the noise – the violent sudden stops and starts that rattled everything moveable – and then there would be the relief of moving on at last with the soothing rhythmical sounds of wheels on rails.

Another fascinating thing about this journey was how these powerful steam engines took on board the necessary water to work efficiently. We observed this by watching the trains coming in the opposite direction on the parallel tracks. There would be a very long trough fixed neatly between the rails, filled with water, and the engines would come along, still at speed, scooping up the water easily with no fuss at all. Then there were specially made contraptions beside the tracks for mailbags too, which could be cleverly swept into the train as it roared by, again without pausing.

We children enjoyed the long corridors of the train itself, running along all the carriages to stretch our legs and watching everything that occurred with great interest. Other passengers were also observing us, it seemed. "Are you twins?" was often their query,

"Tweelings?" This immediately made us feel shy and self-conscious, and these particular people would be carefully avoided in the future!

Having changed trains at De Aar we arrived at last at Mortimer very early in the morning while it was still dark. We hastily climbed out at such a small station where it seemed astonishing that a long and seemingly important train would even deign to notice it. We waited on the platform knowing that the farmer of The Hope was coming to meet us, though Mother seemed to have one or two doubts as we waited for some considerable time. Then, in the far distance, we saw the headlights of a car. Was it coming to Mortimer? The light-beams swung about as corners were turned and as the road, with its dips and little hills, made the lights move up and down. Then the car seemed to disappear altogether for a while only to suddenly reappear very much nearer to us – yes, surely this was the farmer! The car was parked, and a tall man unfolded himself from it and walked towards us.

"Dennis Mahon," he introduced himself, smiling at us all. We told him our names, and soon we were in the car with our luggage (there was not much of this); presently we were swaying and bumping along the road on which we had seen the car with its headlights earlier.

It was just beginning to get light, and we began to see something of the countryside through which we were being driven. There were noticeably very few houses but there were fields (possibly with cereal crops) and trees (mostly, it seemed, firs, pine and eucalyptus). There were fences on either side of rough-looking roads, with gates leading to the few farms scattered about. Here and there we could see little windmills on tall ironwork structures.

Dennis told us that these were where the boreholes had been dug for precious water. This looked quite a desolate place on the whole; it was still part of the veldt on the Karoo, with mainly scrub and salt bushes. Everything looked very dry and dusty. Every now and again we would pass some shabby huts where there were African men, women and children rising at the start of their working day. Here the crops growing were mealies[21] and lucerne, according to Dennis. We drove past some fields with attractive horses grazing. "These are race

---

[21] maize

horses having a rest from their racing," Dennis explained to us children, noticing our immediate interest. Then it became apparent, with the dawning of the sun, that we were driving in the most beautiful valley surrounded with majestic mountains. Presently, when we reached fields with gentle looking cows, he told us, "This is The Hope farm now. These are our cows; they are Jerseys and provide excellent milk rich with cream."

We finally arrived at the main farmhouse of The Hope, sweeping in round a little grassy circle with a few trees growing in the centre. We gazed at it all before opening the car doors – so this is where we were coming to stay! Mrs Mahon, Dennis's mother, came hurrying out to meet us. "How good to see you all," she cried, welcoming us all warmly. Luggage was removed from the car, and Dennis, saying that he would see us again shortly, drove off to his house, which was just out of sight up a slight incline.

Mrs Mahon showed us our bedrooms and told us, "Breakfast will be in the living room as soon as you are ready." We realised we were all quite hungry and joined her swiftly, grateful to have stopped travelling, and enjoyed the peace of such a lovely place. Mrs Mahon invited us children to call her 'Granny Mahon' which made her seem special at once. "My little grandson, Frankie, will be coming down to see you all soon. He always comes in the mornings, and today he knows you are here. He is four years old so he is quite a bit younger than you are." I could tell that he must be very precious to her and that she was very fond of him.

Presently, I could see a fair-haired little boy peering in through the half-glazed door of the living room which led out to the stoep. The early morning sun behind him was shining through his ears, turning them bright red; he looked enchanting and so sweet – I loved him at once. He was quite shy at first, but we were soon to become great friends. Before long we also met his mother, Enid, a very sweet, quiet lady who seemed so kind and gentle.

Granny Mahon had much to tell us about living on the farm. One aspect which we understood well from our recent voyages was the shortage of water and how important it was to conserve it carefully. All the water was obtained by boreholes with little 'windmills' and pumped up to huge corrugated iron tanks. Here the water was stored for the use of the houses, farm buildings and troughs for the animals.

Rainwater was also collected from roofs when possible, but here there would not be much rain for several months at a time; however, there would be times occasionally when fields and gardens would be irrigated from the Tarka River a few miles away. She also explained that we used paraffin lamps and candles and that even the fridge also used paraffin. The lavatory was in the 'little house' outside and quite near the kitchen back-door. This was obviously not a flush toilet, and inside, as we could see, there were two seats with holes carved out of the centres, one of which was quite low for children and the other one slightly higher for grown-ups. There was a strange smell – not really unpleasant, just different. Lindsey and I were reminded of the similar one at 'Lah-Di-Dah' farm.

The telephone, so Mother was told, was a party-line; each farm nearby had its own special signal according to how many bell-rings were heard. I think our phone had nine rings, so each time there was a phone-call we would have to carefully count the number of rings to know if it was a call for our house. The phone was hung on the wall in the little entrance hall and had an earpiece, rather like a trumpet, so that two people could use it together. There was an exchange at Mortimer which could connect the phone for long distance calls when necessary.

The farmhouse was a pleasant one-storey building with the customary stoep arranged on two sides. I realised later that the main one faced south; being south of the equator, this was the cooler side of the house and where it was delightful to sit near the front door, overlooking the entrance drive. The east stoep had a view of the attractive, if rather unkempt, garden, and we discovered that it was on this part of the stoep that Granny Mahon had a large aviary where she kept her budgies and a few canaries. We were amazed at the variety and beauty of their colours. These pretty little birds would need daily attention and were another delight. Granny Mahon also had a dog, a collie, called Jessie and a favourite horse called Bess. We found that Bess would sometimes be tethered to a tree on the circular lawn on the entrance drive. She was a beautiful mare, dark brown with a wonderful sheen in her coat, and she smelt and felt so good to touch!

Lindsey and I found that our bedroom windows looked out onto a large vegetable garden, and this was situated on the north side of the house. Mother's room was next to ours, and besides having a window to the north, she had one facing onto the east-facing stoep and the garden.

We were shown where the cow-byres were and told that we may see the cows being milked and that we may explore the farm buildings, but we were asked not to get in the way of the workers. There was so much to see and explore, and we soon discovered the pen where little calves were kept. They were adorable, and we were thrilled to hear that, perhaps, we could feed them one day. Granny Mahon explained that Dennis' wife, Enid, looked after all the calves, the chickens and the ducks, and that she would probably be glad to have some help at times.

Later, Dennis told us that the cows were milked twice a day, that each would come to the cow-byre knowing exactly which stall to go to, and that they always kept to their own one. He showed us where the milking machines were and said that we may come to the evening milking to see just what happened. I always loved the huge cow-byre. I loved the gentle Jersey cows with their pretty concave faces. I loved the smells of it all and the sense of the peaceful business of men getting on with a well-known routine, the mostly quiet talking (apart for a stern rebuke to some wayward cow), the clanking of machinery and buckets, and the purposefulness of organising the large quantities of wonderful milk and cream, the milk-churns, the churning of butter...

Enid kindly took us to see her Rhode Island Red chickens. First, we concealed ourselves for a little while before they were fed, so that we would not disturb them, and watched with fascination while Enid explained their actions. They lived in what had once been a tennis court; there seemed to be masses of them. It was a scene of great activity and noise, hens scratching in the dust, other hens clucking loudly and triumphantly announcing that an egg had been laid, and cocks strutting proudly about and crowing. When it was time to feed them they became very excited and rushed eagerly to their troughs in a flurry of wings and feathers. Enid collected the beautiful brown eggs carefully into baskets, and I think most of these were sold later.

The ducks wandered about the farmyard and near-by orchard; they were strange-looking Muscovy ducks, and Enid seemed to really love them. They each had their own character and she knew them all.

I thought at first that they were rather ugly, but later, when I realised that each of them was so special, I became quite fond of them too.

Another delight we saw almost immediately was a large heap of sand under a pepper-tree near the backdoor of the kitchen. The road leading to the cow-byres was right by the backdoor steps, and we could walk across this, turning slightly left for the sand and the pepper-tree and right for the 'little-house' with its two seats. The sand was for Frankie to play in, and presently we were all happily busy there together. It was lovely just to be able to do something so simple and pleasurable after our long journey, and I remember beginning to feel relaxed and happy.

I do not quite recall when the following episode happened but I think it was only a few months after our arrival at The Hope. I was with Frankie at his house when I realised it was time to return to ours, perhaps for a meal. It was very hot and Frankie lent me his tricycle, which was really too small for me but fun to ride. I set off down the slope along the track – pausing to look at a gum-tree on the way to see if there was any resin for me to eat and then going gaily on towards our house – when, to my utmost horror, a bright yellow snake came rapidly across my path almost touching the front wheel of the tricycle. I leapt off at once and rushed, screaming with terror, into the cool house.

Granny Mahon appeared and rather sternly asked, "Whatever is the matter?" I replied, with a very shaky voice through my sobs, "I saw a snake, a bright yellow one; it came right up to the tricycle..."

Granny Mahon was amazed that I should make such a fuss. "Well, it didn't hurt you, did it?"

I had to admit that it had not and that it had disappeared very quickly. Mother arrived on the scene and I expected her to be much more sympathetic, but to my surprise she agreed with Granny Mahon; it seemed I had been very foolish to make such a noise. "Mrs Mahon is never afraid of snakes, and she just sees what can be done to get rid of them, killing them if necessary," she explained.

Mother obviously knew something that I did not; my respect for Granny Mahon was enormous. "Fancy," I thought, "not ever being afraid of snakes!" Granny Mahon told me then all sorts of stories of encounters with snakes that she had had, which I found captivating, and realised that I had a great deal to learn. However, I was not wholly convinced that I would ever be able to cope calmly with such alarming reptiles, and I was not sure that I wanted to either!

There were other reptiles, though, which I did enjoy and found endlessly fascinating; these were chameleons, charming little lizard-like creatures which were amazing in the way they changed colour to match their surroundings.

Our first Christmas at The Hope was very different from the previous one; we were with loving people who met joyfully together for a celebratory feast. It was hot. (December is in summer in South Africa, of course.) Dennis, Enid and Frankie joined us, and we all sat round a large table in Granny Mahon's living room; there must have been two other people as well, but now I do not recollect who they were. In a lull during the merry conversation Frankie suddenly remarked, very seriously, "There are nine graves sitting at this table!" There was astonishment all around, and Dennis asked (quite severely, it seemed), "Whatever do you mean, Frankie?"

Frankie, looking quite untroubled, explained sweetly: "Well, everyone here is a grave for the turkey we are eating!" This was a startling thought to each of us!

Our new life on the farm was to prove so interesting with much to discover and to understand, and my sister and I loved it. Mother settled down as best she could; I know it was very hard for her not knowing the whereabouts of Father, or whether he was alive, and to be without him again, but the people in this Christian farming community were wonderfully supportive and showed their care in so many loving ways. Almost everyday someone from another farm would call and, with the Mahons, would pray together for all those whom they knew were involved in the War, naming each of them and asking for God's guidance and protection. It was comforting to know that Father's name was always mentioned in these prayers; this gave us children a great sense of security.

CHAPTER ELEVEN

Tarka Bridge

he Tarka Bridge Community met on Sundays at various venues to worship together; I thought these were very good times, loving the warm friendly fellowship. It was interesting to see the different meeting places and farms. Sometimes we would meet at the Tarka Bridge Training School (for farming), and when I was aged about nine years I was delighted by a sermon I once heard there about an angry father telling his child that God is not real. He wrote in large letters the words for her to see clearly:

GODISNOWHERE

The child read this as, "GOD IS NOW HERE" and was really happy! I was thrilled about the truth of that and loved to think of the presence of Jesus with us – and the angels too! One prayer we always had in these services became increasingly important to me: "...that I may see him more clearly, love him more dearly, and follow him more nearly!"

There was a swimming pool in the grounds; it is true that it had rather murky water, but it was a source of real pleasure. We would try to come here as often as possible as Lindsey and I both loved swimming.

We also used to meet in the Village Hall at Mortimer, where there would be a spread of delicious food! It was here I remember an informal Holy Communion Service in which I just longed to be able to take part; I so wanted to be nearer to Jesus and able to receive the bread and wine, which I realised clearly were a very important part of Christian faith. But I was told that I would have to wait until I was older and felt sad about that. I loved Jesus so much and wanted 'more' of Him! Later it was Eileen Rice who explained to me that people had to be confirmed before they received the bread and the wine. She was so understanding and sweet that I was comforted and realised that I would just have to wait until then.

Eileen was also understanding about my longing to play the piano and to be able to read music; she assured me that when we had a piano of our own and could practise a lot, that would be the time to learn – but, alas, that never happened. We did not ever have a home of our own as I was growing up – or for the first years of marriage![22]

After what must have been a gap of several months Lindsey and I started to go to school again, at the little local school - an interesting experience! It had one teacher for all the ages[23] in one room with the 'little house' outside. In the centre of the school room there was an attractive little stove which, in winter, would throw out a glowing amount of warmth.[24]

There were not many children, and we all came from the various farms within a few miles. Some of us were from the Tarka Bridge Community, and we had the fun of coming to school from the farms by the different wagons being used to provide this transport. The Hope wagon would be drawn by a couple of mules. The Kings (of Daybreak farm) and the Rices had horses. I think another farm had oxen, but while I do not remember all the details now, I have a lovely memory of the Rice's wagon; it had rubber tyres and travelled more smoothly! It was great sitting on the open wagons hanging on tightly

---

[22] Much later, when I was a grandmother, I had an opportunity to learn to play classical guitar and loved it. I continued until we moved away and was no longer near enough to my excellent and very patient teacher to continue with lessons, and missed this very much!

[23] up to about twelve years, if I recall correctly

[24] When Hugh and I visited South Africa on a marvellous holiday in 1997, we called at The Hope farm and met the Boer farmer who then lived there. It was noticeable that he was suspicious of us at first, until I convinced him, quite casually, by speaking about the sulpha spring, knowing it from my childhood! He then kindly invited us in to his house, and amongst other things we saw the actual stove which he had removed from the old tumble-down school building! He was very anxious about the local Africans.

when the rough tracks were extra bumpy. No health and safety rules then!

The old school stove!

The Rice's old wagon, as seen on Hugh's and my visit to Mortimer on a field at their old home. It was recognisable by the rubber tyres!

The ruined Tarka Bridge School Building, 1997, showing some of the beautiful mountains surrounding it.

There was a disadvantage in being such a small school; I think we had a different teacher every term, and I suppose, as she assessed our abilities, we often had to start afresh in several subjects and then, very often, she would have a totally different way of teaching from the previous lady! There are so many ways of teaching arithmetic; it was really confusing! As far as I can tell, there was no set curriculum, and each teacher would just do her best. There was a shortage of books and materials so we often used slates with squeaky 'pencils'.

One interesting Geography lesson I particularly remember was learning how rivers were formed. The teacher got us to make a large pile of sand; someone was told get a pail of water, which she poured out very carefully from above this large 'mountain'; and we could see at once how this made 'rivers' take their courses and keep to the same channels thereafter. It certainly was a helpful demonstration!

I recall another teacher telling us about Psalm 121, which starts off with "I will lift my eyes to the hills." She asked us all to come outside and see the hills round about us. We went outdoors, and I will always remember really looking at these wonderful mountains, realising their beauty, the different blues and purples and the exciting shapes and patterns – and feeling quite awed. She pointed out that the help, which the psalmist spoke about, came from God, not actually the mountains themselves; somehow this psalm meant a great deal to me and is one which I have loved ever since.

Psalm 121 (Authorized Version)
I will lift up mine eyes to the hills, from whence cometh my help. My help cometh from the LORD which made heaven and earth. He will not suffer thy foot to be moved: he that keepeth thee will not slumber. Behold, he that keepeth Israel shall neither slumber nor sleep. The Lord is thy keeper: the LORD is thy shade upon thy right hand. The sun shall not smite thee by day, nor the moon by night. The LORD shall preserve thee from all evil: he shall preserve thy soul. The Lord shall preserve thy going out and thy coming in from this time forth, and even for evermore.

Perhaps it was the same teacher who also taught us to observe the weather, noting down any rainfall, the temperatures and wind directions, and making a chart. I found that very interesting! Is this why, I wonder now, I love to know what the weather is doing every day? This may also have made us aware of the points of the compass and position of the sun.

Different families in turn would give accommodation to the current teacher, one of whom lived with us in The Hope for a term, but I am sorry to say I do not remember much about her. However, later Mother found that one of our teachers was definitely anti-

British, which made it difficult for Lindsey and me. She then decided it was time to find another school for us...

Meanwhile, my greatest joy and interest was life on the farm. I remember once walking quickly to the farm buildings just down the track from our house, hurrying to be at the cow-byres in time to see the cows being milked. I climbed on to the sturdy fence and watched the cows come slowly and purposefully plodding down the rough road from the fields, and waiting in groups to be let into their stalls. The way each cow then went straight to her stall always amazed me; she would quietly take her place and then feed from the trough in front of her. The farm hands set to work at once, going methodically from cow to cow, first wiping the udders and then carefully attaching the milking machines to each teat. The cows hardly seemed to notice and continued munching their fodder contently. The milk spurted along the pipes to the collecting point out of my sight, where everything would be scrupulously clean. I knew that the milk churns would quickly be filled and made ready to take to the roadside at a designated place on a little platform, to await the lorry coming round routinely to all the dairy farms in the area. There were sounds of the clashing and clinking of these metal churns as they were trundled along to the wagon that would carry them all to the main road. These Jersey cows produced a wonderful, creamy milk, very good quality, if not in such quantity as the Friesians from the neighbouring farm. I thought the Jersey cows were really gorgeous with their gentle ways and pretty concave faces, and the beauty of their soft yet varied colouring. I loved their dark eyes and long eyelashes, and realised that each one was an individual with her own personality. There were one or two that I was not so sure about and avoided, but on the whole I found they were sweet and friendly.

On one occasion the Muscovy ducks were in the farmyard, looking hopefully at me for something to eat, but as I did not have any food with me I had to disappoint them all. I wandered into the next shed where there were the separators for cream and watched this process going on. The milk for our homes was already in the jugs to take back presently. Suddenly, I saw a nest with about ten baby mice in it and wondered what to do with them and how to dispose of them quickly. I was filled with dismay at the thought of so many growing up and increasing the unwelcome population of mice in these farm buildings! The ducks were still quacking hopefully outside, and I had a flash thought: perhaps I could give these baby mice to them! I scooped up the tiny creatures and threw them one by one to the ducks who caught them adroitly and swallowed them happily. What a relief! Later, though, I was concerned as to whether that was the best thing to do and felt uneasy; I hoped that these unwelcome offspring had not suffered at all. Perhaps everything happened so quickly for them that they had not had time to even think about it!

I loved it when it was time to feed the little calves near the orchard, and my sister and I were encouraged to help. We would carry the buckets of milk to their pens where Enid would usually be there already, talking to a tiny calf and showing him how to feed from her bucket of fresh, creamy milk. Lindsey and I would each go to the calves we were to feed, trying not to slop the milk about too much. My little calf would be waiting excitedly for me, so I'd lean over the low fence, and gently putting my hand into the milk I would give her a delicious taste of it. Then the calf would eagerly suck my fingers, and as I lowered my hand into the milk again she would find that she could drink it by herself, putting her nose and mouth right into the bucket. She then seemed ecstatically happy, and it gave such pleasure to see her contentment. I liked looking up and seeing the pleased smiles of delight too upon the faces of Enid and Lindsey. This was an enchanting job to do, always.

Granny Mahon had another son living further north and quite often stayed with him and his family for some while. When it was time for her to be with him again, we were happily established and becoming used to our new way of life, and soon Mother was in charge. There were two African 'maids', Jane and Topsy, whom we all liked very much and who were a great help to Mother.

There were many different things for Mother to consider, including her financial situation. She had a regular income from the Hong Kong and Shanghai Bank, but was concerned that there should be enough for when Father returned to us, so she was very careful indeed with any money, being really frugal and trying to live very simply. The Tarka Bridge community were nearly all struggling financially. Farming was not doing very well so everyone, it seemed, was living in the same prudent way; there was no ostentation, no vying over possessions or anything like that, as far as I could see.

There was an attitude of sharing and helping one another and being contented with what one had which, looking back, was inspiring.

Lindsey and I had very few toys or books but loved all that happened on the farm – and enjoyed the marvellous area of deep sand beneath the pepper tree. Here we played very happily with Frankie, using our vivid imaginations creatively. We all liked making 'sand farms' with fields and buildings, and having so little in the way of toys, we discovered that you could use pinecones for the different animals – tiny ones for the sheep and larger ones for cattle, mules, oxen or donkeys. We eagerly sought cones that had upturned stalks, which are very good for representing horses or oxen, and can be harnessed satisfactorily to tiny 'carts' or 'wagons'. We enjoyed making roads and planning the layout of little farms or even villages.

There were no shops anywhere near The Hope, and it was quite an event once a week when each farm in turn sent a wagon to do the shopping at Mortimer, some six miles away. With no other transport Mother found this system very useful. She had to have a list of everything that might be required for the coming week and the necessary money ready to pay for it. She was not a very organised person and found it hard to plan ahead, but she tried not to forget any essentials. The list consisted of articles not found on the farm – sometimes flour, a large 8lb tin of golden syrup[25], coffee, tea, biscuits (Mother liked Rich Tea biscuits best), sugar (usually hard to get but worth a request), oil for the lamps, candles, matches, lavatory paper, soap[26]… Mother would write it all down carefully and look forward to the arrival of the wagon.

One of my favourite places was in the pepper-tree. I loved being able to climb into it as high as I could, brushing aside the leafy fronds with the hanging bunches of attractive peppers, feeling a bit secluded and enjoying a moment on my own. I recall that on one particular day I wondered which of the wagons would be coming. I started to daydream… If I had a wagon, I thought, I would choose to have the one with the beautiful Percheron horses, but those horses might be too big and tall for me to harness. I didn't fancy the mules so much or

---

[25] "That is about the weight of a good-sized newborn baby," I heard once, and somehow the thought delighted me.

[26] The same sort of soap would be needed for both the bathroom and the kitchen. There were no detergents in those days.

the oxen, but perhaps the sixteen little donkeys would be best. Yes, I thought, I could manage those, and it would be fun to catch each of them and put on their tiny harnesses for the wagon. What would I call them all? There were endless possibilities, and then I remembered Mother's flowery names for her fictitious daughters and dreamily enjoyed choosing sixteen names: Rosie, Iris, Violet, Petunia, Marigold, Poppy, Jasmine... My reverie ceased abruptly; I could hear the noise and creaking of a wagon approaching. First there was the sound of the old gate opening, with a bit of a squeak, at the entrance of the pear-tree avenue leading to the house. Then I heard the 'boys' calling to the oxen, the slashing of whips, and the slow plodding of hooves coming nearer. I quickly scrambled down the tree and stood at the kitchen door ready for the wagon's arrival. A span of eight oxen hitched to the wagon of the neighbouring farm came majestically into view and halted at the steps leading up to the kitchen. Eight sleek, reddish brown, shiny-coated animals with yokes on their necks were hitched to the old wagon. "It is a bit difficult to make friends with oxen," I sighed, somewhat disappointedly, "but they are so shiny and beautiful." I patted the nearest one – who didn't seem to respond at all.

The men made cheerful remarks, and taking Mother's shopping-list from Jane, they encouraged the oxen, very loudly, with more cracking of whips, to start again, and the wagon moved off ponderously. It would stop at 'Daybreak' next, the farm belonging to the Kings, where Eileen, my eight-year-old friend, would also be eagerly waiting; then it would continue on to the Rices before reaching Mortimer and the shop, where the oxen would be out-spanned and given a well-deserved rest.

Lindsey joined me, and we decided to play in the huge pile of sand beneath the pepper-tree with Frankie. There we had fun re-enacting the morning's shopping expedition with the oxen – eight little cones hitched to the larger cone 'wagon'. Soon Mother called us for lunch, and we could hear Enid calling Frankie for the same reason. Frankie obediently ran to 'The Birdcage', as everyone calls his fly-proofed house. (It was called this because it had a fly-proof, light wire netting, rather like gauze, all round the outside of the verandahs encircling the house.) We found that our lunch consisted of ham from one of the farm's own pigs and vegetables from the garden. The food was always so good with all the fresh produce from the farm; it was an excellent diet. Living on a dairy farm meant that we had a marvellous supply of milk, cream and eggs, and always an abundance of fresh meat. We hardly ever had sweets, but when possible we would chew delicious sticks of sugar-cane straight from the fields – such a treat.

It was a hot day, pleasantly so, and Mother suggested that Lindsey and I take some clothes, mostly small items, to wash at the spring. This was a sulphur spring within a short distance of the house; although it reeked of the smell of rotten eggs, it was fun to go there. We took the basket of clothes and walked down the path with its thorn bushes and other prickly shrubs on either side. There was something mysterious about this track which we only half-liked. It was overshadowed by trees and rather dark, but the water bubbled up from the spring and flowed away so attractively. It was great to get the clothes really soapy and then to scrub them hard, seeing how clean we could get them; this was very satisfying. We then soon found other interesting things to do, so with damming up the spring and making little stepping-stones across the stream, we thoroughly enjoyed ourselves.

After some while we returned to the house in time to see that Mother had had visitors. We hung the washing out to dry, saying to each other that we should have guessed that something was happening because we were often sent on errands when Mother wanted to talk to someone on her own. I remember feeling a little sad, wondering if Mother was distressed about some news, perhaps about Father and the War.

Every morning the Mahons came to discuss the latest war situation; they looked earnestly at the large map of the world on the living room wall and talked about 'fronts'. I found the war situation so hard to understand, but the adults used to say that it was best for us children to leave it all to them, and I felt reassured knowing that there was much prayer, not only for Father but about all the War too.

Later, we heard the wagon noisily returning, well-laden with shopping and supplies for the farms. The oxen looked quite hot, but the 'boys' were as cheerful as ever. After a brief stop, the wagon departed, creaking and groaning, to the last farm and the end of the day's expedition. Lindsey and I dashed to the kitchen steps again and helped to carry in the parcels for Mother. It was always so interesting to unpack the bundles and find what we had on these occasions. That day Mother was delighted to see, amongst all the other things, that there was some sugar, and planned to make a cake soon. This was a rare pleasure, and an eager discussion ensued as to what the flavour should be – orange, chocolate or Madeira. Sometimes we were allowed to help and we very much enjoyed the opportunity. I was always amazed at the way the wet mixture in the bowl, after all the efforts of beating the eggs and butter with a spoon, would actually become a dry and delicious cake, smelling marvellous as it was taken out of the oven.

The day was drawing to a close and it became cooler. Mother prepared the lamps that we would need, making certain they were filled sufficiently with paraffin, and also set candles in their holders where necessary.

I made sure that there were enough dry fir cones to light the fire with, so presently we had the pleasure of sitting cosily around a blazing fire, the wood crackling, spitting and still smoking a little, the paraffin lamps gently hissing and causing any objects nearby to send out long, dancing shadows onto the walls.

"Now, where are we in our story?" Mother asked, picking up the book 'Water-Babies' and turning the pages. Mother read aloud very well but found that this somehow made her yawn, which I thought rather distracting. But I loved those evenings in that peaceful room, and I remember looking round it appreciatively. There was a little rug at our feet and a favourite picture on the wall, which Mother had managed to bring from Malaya. "Just a few things that help to make a home again," she had said, when arranging them carefully. Soon we were all deeply into the story, feeling for the different characters and indignant at the injustices. Every now and again, we would put another log onto the fire and enjoy the renewal of the spitting and crackling which immediately occurred.

"Time for bed," Mother suddenly announced very firmly, breaking off in what seemed a most exciting place. It was no use protesting so Lindsey and I each took a candle, lighting these from the fire, for the cold bedroom which we shared and to prepare for the night. But first, I peeped out of the sitting room to see if the moon was shining and was delighted to find that it was. I recall that I looked at 'my' pepper-tree and admired the beautiful shadow-shapes that the moonlight made on the sandy place beneath. Then I wandered into the bathroom with my candle flickering so much that it was in danger of going out and placed it carefully on its special stand. It gave enough light to brush my teeth and to wash my face and hands. No bath that night because I was aware that we must use very little water as the big water storage tank outside the kitchen door was worryingly low.

Mother lovingly tucked us up and said prayers with us both before returning to the warm fireside. After such a lovely day, I relaxed contently and listened to the sounds of the night, the dogs barking in the distance and an owl hooting. Lindsey and I whispered a little to each other sleepily and, becoming very drowsy, soon fell fast asleep.

CHAPTER TWELVE

Littlefield

*L*ife continued happily for my sister and me, but Mother always grieved very much over Father, although continuing to be so courageous in her trust in God for her dear husband. It must have seemed in a way that she was neither wife nor widow; it was very hard that there was no news either about him or, of course, from him. Thankfully no one knew then about the appalling conditions that the Prisoners of War were suffering in the prisons and camps under the Japanese in the Far East; I think we would have felt dreadful being totally incapable to help him.

Lindsey and I continued going to Tarka Bridge School, enjoying the farm life and getting to know the people on neighbouring farms. There were the kindly Bautchers on the nearest farm, where I remember having fun washing hair. Amy would set out several basins of clean water on a bench out in the warm sunshine, and we would go swiftly from one to the other for the various stages of washing and rinsing! We also learnt about 'biltong' – meat that had been dried in the sun and was delicious – and more about the South African way of life. There was a little African boy there whom we saw sometimes, who had tribal mark scars on his head; it was so interesting to begin to understand these customs first-hand from those who knew so much about the African way of life.

The Kings of Daybreak farm were another family we got to know quite well. They had two children – Eileen, who was about our age, and her younger, rather tiresome little brother, who annoyed most people with his mischief; I recall the upset he caused by putting sand into the petrol tank of Dennis Mahon's car! We loved going to this farm where they kept the huge and beautiful Percheron horses. It was great in the stables, where we all enjoyed playing on the hay bales, stacked up to almost the height of the ceiling in one of the barns, climbing up and then scampering along them before a rapid and slippery descent.

We were invited to Daybreak one Sunday for lunch; it was a delicious roast chicken, and I was excited to win the wishbone. Everyone encouraged me to make a secret wish, telling me that I could ask for anything I wanted and that I would be sure to have my wish! I thought hard about this, wondering what I wanted most of all, and realised clearly that I longed to have Father with us more than anything else in the world. However, I decided not just to make a wish but to pray specifically again. Knowing that God answers earnest prayers, I slipped away to be on my own. I found this special moment was amazingly comforting and knew that God really had heard my heartfelt prayer and that He was in charge of Father and our situation too!

The farm beyond that of Barton King belonged to Captain Rice and his wife Eileen. It was a stud farm where they had many lovely horses and where other racehorses would come for a rest. Captain Rice, as he was always known, was a strict disciplinarian, and I was a bit scared of him; but we discovered he was really thoughtful and kind under his brusque exterior. He realised we loved horses and suggested that we learnt to ride! We were thrilled and loved going there for our lessons, even though it could be quite painful riding bareback!

Later he found us a pony each, little Basuto ponies, probably already quite old, and we loved them dearly. Lindsey's was called Tom, a bit livelier than mine but he had a vicious bite at times! Mine was called Charlie, whom I adored and immediately named Bonnie Prince Charlie, of course! He was so gentle and had wonderfully melting, brown eyes. As soon as we were considered proficient enough, we were able to ride them back to The Hope, where Dennis Mahon gave us a paddock to keep them in. We would return to the Rice's and join in with the rides there sometimes, and got to know the roads and tracks round about quite well. We also were able to go swimming at the Training School farm in the other direction, riding near the Tarka River and finding the track which led to the pool. Occasionally we rode to our school but didn't like having to tether the ponies there for long.

Gymkhanas were held regularly somewhere near Mortimer, and these were always wonderful events. We had such fun watching the races and thoroughly enjoyed it all, even though we were not ready to participate, nor were our ponies nearly good enough to compete with such excellent horses. I particularly loved the 'Wag-n-Bikkie'[27] race, when riders rode other competitors' horses, wanting theirs to be the last one at the finishing post! This actually meant it was the fastest race of all!

Then came a special day for all the farmers when their fields were to be irrigated. This was quite an event; water from the Tarka River was channelled to the many irrigation channels and would gently flow along with a series of little gates, allowing precious water into the chosen fields and even gardens. It was amazing to observe how well this worked and then, later, to see how the crops would respond. I remember when the water flowed into our vegetable garden and how exciting this seemed!

Another time I recall was making 'cigarettes' in this vegetable garden; Lindsey and I noticed that everyone seemed to smoke so we thought we would try this out one day. Finding some suitable material, little sticks of some sort perhaps, we lit them and started to puff away – but it was horrid, and choking uncomfortably we soon decided that that was most unpleasant and not for us after all! Neither of us ever smoked again; maybe this was just as well!

Another thing we did enjoy was when crops where brought in from the fields and we were allowed by the kind farm hands to climb on to the top of these heavily loaded wagons. I remember how I loved swaying along (a little precariously) on the slightly slippery load of mealies once, seeing everything from a very different perspective.

We still had such fun with playing with Frankie and used to make little 'houses' in amongst bushes and shrubs near the sandpit. One of the things I always insisted on having in my 'houses' was a sideboard; I had seen one in the Rice's home and thought it must be a very special piece of furniture; now I have had my very own one for

---

[27] Wait-a-Bit, in Afrikaans

several decades – and still like it! Frankie had some little playhouses outside his Birdcage House, and once when there were enchanting kittens, we had such fun with these delightful little pets, allowing them to play in them too.

Frankie was growing up, and when he was about five, I had a wonderful time teaching him to begin to read. I felt this was such a privilege and thought that he was a marvellous pupil!

I always loved the way his Dad, Dennis, would call him "my little man", picking him up and carrying him on his shoulders. Dennis called Enid, his sweet wife, "my Princess", and I loved that too (although, wistfully, I longed to have a father who would love us like that!)

Mother decided that she would invite any people from army personnel who needed a holiday. Various people would come, and this was usually very pleasant; however, one family arrived with a young boy whom I did not like at all! Understandably, he was not used to being on a farm, but we did not care for his rough ways – he was so insensitive! One day he accused me of smashing every one of Martha's eggs. Now Martha was one of the dear Muscovy ducks for whom I cared deeply and watched happily as she brooded several eggs. It was most distressing to see the broken eggs anyway, and I was very upset by this false accusation – and then surprised that Mother did not firmly support me. I think she was aware that this family were our guests and, perhaps, did not want a fuss.

So I prayed about this great unhappiness. By this time, in my imagination, I had made a 'little cabin' attached to the outside wall of the Tarka Bridge School. It was a very simple whitewashed building, and this was my 'special place' where I would meet with my Lord Jesus and just enjoy being in His company. It was here that I went in my distress, and to my relief I realised that He was reassuring me that He was the truth, that nothing could ever alter the truth, and that He is the *absolute* truth! So He knew and understood – and that was so healing and wonderful! This is a truth that even now, sometimes, makes such a difference to me; false accusations are just that – merely false!

Mother also had some lovely naval people to stay; two of the young men, aged about nineteen, made a great impression – and they enjoyed our ponies too. One of these sailors was Tony Ames, and at the age of nine I fell very much in love with him! He was handsome, kind, and fun-loving, and I thought he was the most special man that had ever lived! I found I could really talk with him surprisingly easily and liked his friendship. He and his friend, who I think was called Tom, seemed to come quite often and were popular with us all. But years later Mother told me that Tony was very attracted to Amy Bautcher's daughter at the next farm; I am glad I didn't know that at the time!

Mother cared very much for people in the armed forces – and learnt how to spin wool so that she could knit socks and pullovers for the men. There was an old spinning wheel on the farm, and I admired the clever way the wool from sheep on a neighbouring farm could be spun, made into skeins which were then wound into the balls from which to knit the various garments. I liked to be able to help a bit in this and thought Mother was wonderful in all she tried to do for such needy people. Sometimes she would pause in her spinning or knitting to watch the birds around the garden; this was always a joy to her and an interest throughout her life. She was thrilled with each beautiful or unusual bird that suddenly appeared, pointing them out to us and very often being able to name them.

At about this time Mother was asked if she would take a lodger who was recovering from a serious illness, Arthur Pillinger. She willingly agreed, happy to try to repay the kindnesses she had gratefully found at The Hope. Arthur stayed for quite a while and they became good friends. I am not sure when, but it was while we were away on a rare holiday in Port Elizabeth staying in a hotel near the sea that Mother heard the sad news about my pony, Bonnie Prince Charlie. He had eaten something poisonous and died... I was heart-broken! Mother comforted me by saying that as he was such a loved pony he would now be galloping about very happily indeed in Heaven and that I would see him again when it was the right time for me. I believed her thankfully and found this a most reassuring thought!

Mother became increasingly concerned about our schooling and had several discussions with Eileen Rice, who was a special friend. Eileen told her of a very small school quite nearby, on the farm called 'Littlefield', which might have been ideal. Arthur and Helen, whose surname I cannot remember now, had a young daughter, Margaret, aged about seven. They had arranged for a governess, Miss Wyatt, to come from England to tutor her. They would often have other children staying in their house to join in with the lessons, so each child would have a lot of individual help and attention. It sounded so good, and Eileen arranged for the three of us to visit Arthur and Helen and see this little school. We were all rather impressed with the lovely amenities on the farm; there was a swimming pool, delightful places round about for children to play, opportunities for riding, and a sweet little schoolroom in the rondavel[28]. The 'little house' was just outside the back door of the main house in an orchard. The pupils had bedrooms in the house, and meals were served in an attractive dining-room. So, Mother decided that this was to be our next school.

In the meanwhile, Mother had thought very much about our financial position and felt that the time had come for her to find a paid job. As Arthur Pillinger was making excellent progress she applied to become Matron at a boy's school in Grahamstown; this was Fairlawn, St Andrew's Prep School. She found this to be quite a difficult challenge, again having to settle in a new area not knowing anyone and doing unfamiliar work. Arthur, who though much improved was still quite frail, continued to live at The Hope. It may have been at this point that Mother bought a car, which proved to be a great asset – a much loved, rather elderly Rover with a 'running-board'.

Enid and Dennis were expecting a new baby, and there was much joy when Geraldine was born. Mother was asked to be her godmother and was delighted. She loved to help Enid, and I remember her pleasure in having this sweet little baby to stay and assisting her to sleep through the night! It was difficult to leave 'The Hope' for school at this point and missing the excitement of this new baby, but later we were thrilled when we were able to come back on holidays and could see her for ourselves.

Lindsey and I must have been aged about ten by now, and we went confidently off to 'Littlefield' for another stage in our lives. We found that we had an attractive bedroom to share, with a beautiful view across the valley to the familiar blue/purple mountains where, sometimes, we could hear the train on its way from Mortimer to

---

[28] a small African-type, round building

Cradock away in the distance. We were rather shy at first; there were only six of us, all girls, including Margaret, the farmer's daughter, but somehow it seemed difficult to make friends. We were the oldest children and were given a table for just the two of us in the dining-room, everyone else being seated at a large, round table. There were new ways to get accustomed to, of course, and some new rules.

There was something about Littlefield which undermined our confidence. Perhaps it was that Margaret was so obviously her parents' favourite and we were just the oldest girls, but while it had everything going for it on the surface there was some sort of an undercurrent which I know made us unhappy. I loved the riding though; we would rise very early and find the beautiful ponies all saddled and ready to ride, and we enjoyed these rides very much with Miss Wyatt. My favourite pony was 'Silver-Grey', and while I remained loyal to the memory of Bonnie Prince Charlie, I really loved her too! I think Miss Wyatt was an unhappy person, and perhaps she only came to life when riding her favourite horse named 'Helmet' – I just don't know. She did not encourage us in our lessons, and I think we were made to feel we were failures! Uncle Arthur was so kind and we liked him very much, but he wasn't always there, of course. Aunt Helen seemed austere and not loving, and I was wary of her.

But there were many things which we *did* enjoy very much. There were lambs that needed feeding, who were so sweet, and playful kittens too. However, there was an occasion when Lindsey was accused of causing harm to one of the kittens; we were very indignant. I knew Lindsey loved the kittens and would never, ever hurt one! This was so distressing! On the other hand, I liked it particularly when, occasionally, Uncle Arthur organised a 'lantern display', rather like photo slides which would be projected onto a wall – a new and fascinating experience. Sometimes he would take one of us to be a 'gate-opener' for him when he had to visit another farm quite a long way from Littlefield, and this was a great treat. The idea was that a child could jump out of the vehicle and open the gates on the various farm roads for the driver to pass through. I also enjoyed having our suppers on the stoep every evening; these would all be attractively arranged on a tray with delicious things such as biscuits with cheese and several varieties of fruit.

It's alright now – God is in charge!

Miss Wyatt taught us to learn poems, or sometimes prose, by heart. We had never done this before, and I found that Tennyson's poem 'The Brook' was wonderful. Lindsey learnt Psalm Eight; everyone had something to contribute to a little event Miss Wyatt arranged for friends and neighbours. Mother was not able to come, but I know Eileen Rice came with her son, Dick, of about our age, who was another special friend of ours. I believe Eileen realised that we were not very happy, and she was concerned. Afterwards, she told Mother, confessing that she felt rather responsible (I think) because other children who had been at Littlefield had not been happy either, and she wondered if this was something to do with Aunt Helen.[29]

When riding one day, a little dog followed us back to Littlefield and seemed to attach himself particularly to me. I was very flattered and just loved this small, white dog – a mongrel with possibly some Fox Terrier in him. He was white with lots of little darkish marks on him, and I named him Freckles. It must have been at the end of term, and when Dennis kindly came to collect us in his car, to my astonishment, this little dog followed us all the way back to The Hope. He became a very dear friend!

Lindsey was having some trouble with her nose and breathing, and Mother made an appointment for her to see a doctor in Port Elizabeth, leaving me in the care of Arthur. While I realised that Freckles must belong to somebody else, it meant a lot to me that I had his companionship too. But you can imagine my dismay when one day a very rough-looking man turned up on horseback at our house, demanding to have his dog back; he meant 'my' darling dog! He must have heard that he was with us somehow, and putting poor, unwilling little Freckles into a sack fixed in front of his saddle, he rode off with him! It would have made such a difference if I knew Freckles was really cared for! I never saw him after that and was heartbroken again; I was so grateful to Arthur who sweetly tried to comfort me. I wrote to Penny telling her about this, and fairly recently I discovered that she had kept this letter for a great many years!

---

[29] Strangely, when Hugh and I returned to visit Mortimer in 1997 and we saw the road leading to Littlefield with its name on the gate, I shrank from it and just did not want to see the place again!

Arthur was wonderful with children and I know, in his gentle way, taught me a lot. I would have loved him as my teacher always! When Mother and Lindsey were due to return from Port Elizabeth, he suggested that we made a 'welcome home' present for them, so we had a lovely time deciding what this would be. In the end it was to gather flowers, pretty little violets, and arrange them in a basket which he showed me how to make.

I am not sure quite when, but sometime later on Lindsey had serious food-poisoning at Littlefield and there was much concern for her. She returned to The Hope to recuperate, and it seemed there was indignation for the way she had been treated. Still working at St Andrews Prep School, Mother decided it was time to find yet another school for us; this time it would be in Grahamstown!

There was much discussion and prayer amongst Mother and her dear friends of the Tarka Bridge Community, and presently, Mother found that The Victorian Girls High School in Grahamstown could take us as their new pupils, so plans were made accordingly. Another stage of our lives was about to begin in Grahamstown, a town and a very different place from our beloved Karoo. We would so miss the veldt, the brilliant stars at night, the mountains, The Hope and the Tarka Bridge Community; but, thankfully, we had the certainty that God was still in charge and prayerfully were sure that all would be well![30]

---

[30] The Mahons were going through quite a lot of difficulties at this time, as I have seen from old letters written to Mother. They were wondering about returning to England, and Dennis told her about the problems of selling The Hope and of mixed feelings, mostly of sorrow, in leaving Tarka Bridge and the people there. Here is a quote from Dennis' letter addressed to Mother in 1944: *"... When I think of your faith in all your trials and on the whole the wonderful upholding through a long, delayed fulfillment, I feel my faith to be very feeble. I do know it will be for the best in the end [referring to the hoped-for sale of his farm], and we will not be forgotten ever, but also we mustn't do anything wildly. Whatever happens, I will always be grateful to you for your kindness to Enid and myself, your talks, example, and the daily prayers. The readings from all parts of the Bible widened and refreshed one's knowledge ... With love from Enid and Frankie, our prayers and best wishes, and may you soon get good news."*

CHAPTER THIRTEEN

Grahamstown

*T*here were mixed feelings in all of us as we left Mortimer and those wonderful people who had become as family to us all, and yet it was exciting to come to Grahamstown and begin, yet again, another new phase in our lives.

Mother, having worked at the St Andrew's Prep School in Grahamstown, had some new friends who, again, were very good to her. She worshipped at St Michael and St George's Cathedral and must have met many kind people there as well. I know that one particular family took her under their wing, so to speak; these were Norman and Effie Favell and their daughter, Margaret, who lived on Stones Hill just south east of Grahamstown. We were all invited to stay with them in their very pleasant house and were here for quite a considerable time – and very much appreciated their loving hospitality. Norman had a large and handsome dog, a Doberman Pincher, with whom Lindsey and I soon became friends too.

The house had the usual stoep which was the main living area. It had a fly-proof door leading into the sitting room; this was attractively furnished, and it was here that Norman kept, amongst many other things, his Geographical Magazines which always fascinated me and taught me a lot! Mother had a bedroom off the sitting room which she shared with Lindsey, and I had a little room on the other side of the house which I loved, thoroughly enjoying a little independence.

There was an attractive garden with a large lawn in the front, edged by trees, beyond which was a lovely view over the hillside towards Grahamstown and the hills on the other side of the valley. This was quite a large property with a vegetable garden and lots of fruit, including strawberries, raspberries and fig trees. Norman kept a cow (or two?) and there were servants helping to run everything efficiently. My impression was of neatness and order everywhere and a kindly man who knew how to organise things well.

Effie was a loving, very gentle lady, who seemed to have an air of sorrow about her, I thought. Much later I realised that Margaret, their daughter, had a learning difficulty and was not very easy to relate to – perhaps that was the cause of the sadness. Norman and Effie hoped so much that she would marry and have a family. Maybe that was partly why they somehow took so lovingly to us, making us feel we were part of their family.

Mother would take us to St Michael and St George's Cathedral for services on Sundays. This is an imposing building in the centre of Grahamstown, right on the High Street. I thought the services there were a bit remote after the close fellowship of the Tarka Bridge Community ones, but there was a dignified liturgy which I began to enjoy.

Grahamstown Cathedral (centre left)
and VGHS buildings in foreground (1997)

It's alright now – God is in charge!

Lindsey and I started to go to Victoria Girls' High School in Grahamstown. We found this to be an enormous school of about six hundred girls, with classes of about thirty pupils. We all had to wear a navy-blue uniform, and it took us both a while to adjust to this whole new situation. Lessons were interestingly different, and I think, on the whole, we found them alright – that is, except for 'Hygiene', which seemed to be a very important subject at this school. To our horror it was taken entirely in Afrikaans! We just did not know anything like enough; I was very embarrassed to discover that one of my exam results was 4%, and I have an awful feeling that Lindsey's marks were no better!

There was a swimming pool which pleased us very much, a Drama Society, which I joined later on and found it to be an interesting experience, and an Art Club – here I drew endless ponies, missing our Basuto ponies and all the riding so much. But there seemed quite a lot going on which was enjoyable and new to us.

Our form used to go to classes at a Training School for Teachers nearby, run by some wonderful nuns.[31] I liked the atmosphere; there was a real incentive to learn and an encouraging enthusiasm with a genuine interest in the pupils. It was set in some beautiful grounds, and with many unusual plants and trees there was always so much to see!

After some while Mother found a small bungalow, still on Stones Hill, quite near to the Favells, and we moved in, finding it good to be a little family on our own again. There was the familiar 'little house' outside and a rather untidy garden. Mother soon became friends with our neighbours who were the nuns in charge of the Training School attached to their convent. After a while they very kindly gave us a lift to our school in the mornings on the way to their Mother House in Grahamstown; this was such a help to Mother.

Lindsey and I were not really aware of it at the time but Mother had a recurrence of Tuberculosis, and when this was diagnosed she was firmly advised to have treatment at a sanatorium some distance away. I think she did not want to alarm us by discussing this illness, but everything seemed to happen so quickly and we very suddenly

---

[31] Recently I had the joy of meeting the retired Mother of this order when she was visiting the UK from Grahamstown and learnt how their work is continuing, although now in several different ways.

had to go to the Boarding House, in Somerset Road, for VGHS girls. This was a great shock to us! We were so unprepared and so was Dorset House, the Boarding House, who gave us a room which may have been the sickbay! I remember being completely dismayed on finding that no soap had been provided and that, apparently, we should have brought our own!

We did settle down but it seemed to take a long time, and I don't think we were really happy there. Mother was in a sanatorium somewhere in the country, but it must have been a very difficult time for her as well. I just knew that everything was suddenly so different, and I did not quite understand what was happening.

We used to have a little evensong with prayers after supper at Dorset House, and I think that helped a bit. We would sing hymns, some of which I already knew and loved, and I liked it particularly when we sang the hymn 'Eternal Father, strong to save' with the words "O hear us when we cry to Thee for those in peril on the sea" because I always thought of my sailor friend, Tony, and prayed earnestly for his safety!

Lindsey and I used to make signals to each other at meals sometimes, especially when I thought she was reprimanded for something really trivial. I would twist my fingers in a particular way behind my back as she walked behind me so that she could see my sympathy! And she would do the same for me! One night, in our dormitory with several other girls, I was woken very roughly by the staff on duty, demanding to know where Lindsey was. She had somehow disappeared, much to everyone's alarm, but I couldn't help because I did not know either, and was not believed; she was my twin sister so it was 'obvious' that I should have known! Actually I do not remember now what happened, but it could not have been too drastic!

Mother gradually recovered and was able to return home, but it was felt to be best that we should stay on at Dorset House, perhaps to allow her to recuperate. I am not sure that we ever talked very much about this episode; after a while it probably just seemed a normal part of life.

At some point, I had to have a tonsillectomy and was whisked into the Grahamstown hospital. I thought this might be a wonderful experience and felt rather important in a large ward mostly with

117

adult ladies. I was rather surprised when one of the busy nurses started swabbing my side with bright yellow iodine, so I asked with great interest if this is what happens when you have your tonsils out. She was mortified, saying quickly that she thought I was having my appendix out! The staff were all very nice to me, and then the time came when I was wheeled into the theatre, still feeling fairly confident, although a little apprehensive about the unknown experience of any operation.

All seemed well until a terrifying mask was put over my face and I had to breathe in the horrible chloroform! Thankfully it is not like this at all nowadays! But it was a very nasty experience; I felt betrayed, I couldn't breathe and struggled in utter terror until, mercifully, I lost consciousness! Then I had the very unpleasant coming round to find such pain... Mother came to collect me from the hospital and then the old Rover car broke down! The whole memory of my tonsillectomy experience became a blur, and it certainly was one I wanted to forget forever!

However, when I had recovered sufficiently, Mother took me to the Favells' lovely little seaside cottage at Kenton; this was about eighty miles further south. We had stayed there previously, and we always liked it very much. It was unusual to have Mother all to myself and I enjoyed this too! We had lots of opportunities to talk, and I felt I grew even closer to her. I think it was a good time of recovery for Mother too; she seemed to do a lot of reading and resting. It must have been the short school holiday just then so there were plans for Lindsey to visit The Hope, travelling with some friends of Mother's.

Everyone in England seems rather shocked when I tell of the times we used to catch fleas! Kenton seemed to have rather a lot of these! Stretching out a blanket from a bed Mother and I would take a tablet of soap, wet it slightly from a bowl of hot water, and looking very intently, examining every part of the blanket carefully, we would pounce on any flea we saw. It would stick to the soap in a very satisfactory way and then be easily disposed of by drowning in the hot water. It could become quite a skill with practice and seemed just a natural part of life!

Presently I began to be much better and would love to wander along the sand dunes covered with rough, spikey grasses, down to the beach. When I reached the shore I would walk along carefully watching out for any 'bluebottles', the bright blue sea creatures that sometimes got washed up with the high tides; these had long strands with little blue swellings which could sting and were best avoided! I enjoyed exploring the rocks on the east side of Kenton Bay and gazing into the different world of small and busy sea creatures, so at home in their little rock pools.

I would happily spend time just absorbing the beauty of this lovely area, feeling a real part of it in a lovely way, and knowing the presence of God. This was a great joy and very healing in many ways. I loved feeling the wind in my hair, the sun on my back, and watching the gulls in graceful flight; I loved the pounding of the waves roaring up onto the beach and rejoiced in feeling wonderfully relaxed and free and deeply content.

Then, we had a worrying phone call; Lindsey, with Mother's friends, had had a car accident on their return from Mortimer. Naturally Mother was very concerned; we hurriedly cut short our little holiday and drove back to Grahamstown where we found Lindsey a bit shaken and frightened, but thankfully alright.

Soon it was the beginning of a new term, and I returned to VGHS and Dorset House while Lindsey recovered from the accident, being with Mother on her own too... It was the first time I had been at school without Lindsey, and it seemed strange at first. I remember clearly that I was very tanned from my seaside holiday and watched my skin peeling with fascination! Lindsey returned to school shortly, and life seemed to return to normality.

The following are a hotchpotch of memories that stand out at VGHS and Dorset House. I remember especially we had made a friend who was a day-girl and had fun with her, writing little notes to each other and hiding them under a particular stone at the entrance of Dorset House. It was a delightful thing to do, particularly as it was rather secretive!

At the boarding house we tried to play hockey, improvising the rules and using whatever suitable stick we could find. There always seemed plenty to do in any free time, and it was fun to be with several other children. Including us, there were three sets of identical twins, all at different ages; I do not think we had met other twins before.

It's alright now – God is in charge!

Dorset House was very cold in winter, and once there was even a little snow (well, just a few flakes, which was exciting!) But there were not enough blankets and it was really cold at night! And then the summers were very hot and it was hard to keep cool. I remember the girls would try keeping wrists cool in running water, helpfully advising that this would make all the difference!

It was quite a walk to the school from the boarding house, and we used to have to obediently go along in 'crocodile formation'. We also had to line up at the main school to go to Assembly in the mornings, and in the Hall we would all form our various 'houses' in long columns. There were six of these, all named after famous women; Lindsey's house was 'Jenny Lind', with small, brown-coloured badges to wear, and mine was 'Ellen Terry', with purple badges – but I do not now remember all the other house names!

Once there was a dental inspection at school, and I was surprised that when my teeth were scrutinized carefully I was asked who my dentist was because a filling had been done so beautifully – and I think that must have been done in Singapore by the Chinese dentist! We were both asked in an English class once to say some words in English – words such as 'Saturday' and 'brown cow' and a few others – and to my amazement everyone had to try to repeat these words just as we had pronounced them! Then there was a dance at the school which seemed to be great fun for the older girls especially. I think at the time we were too junior to take much part, but I was impressed with one particular dance when either a boy or a girl had to just partner a broom; that seemed to be hilarious, and I began to really look forward to joining in one day!

I enjoyed the play that the Drama Club produced. I had a very small role – that of a Queen Mother – but I liked the rehearsals and the costumes and the exhilaration everyone felt when we actually performed. I must have been one of the youngest girls, and I think it was a good experience for me even though I was so shy. I wonder sometimes if I would have liked to have done more drama later on, had there been another opportunity; on the other hand, as I am not good at learning by heart, it may not have been such a great idea! There were several other schools competing from Grahamstown besides VGHS, and ours didn't win the cup after all!

As a family we would often talk about Father, Mother always keeping a great interest in the news bulletins, of course. We received just three treasured postcards from Father during the three and a half years that he was imprisoned – awful, uninformative, impersonal POW cards from the Japanese camps, with no real news. Each card would arrive about eighteen months after it was sent so we did not know, by the time it eventually arrived, if he was still alive. Mother did not discuss this with us, but I realise that receiving these postcards was a bitter/sweet experience in many ways.

IMPERIAL JAPANESE ARMY

Date 23 / 1 / 1944

Your mails (and OTHERS') are received with thanks.
My health is (good, ~~usual, poor~~).
~~I am ill in hospital.~~
I am working for pay (~~I am paid monthly salary~~).
~~I am not working.~~
My best regards to SHEILA PADDY LINDSEY MOTHER SAL HARRY

VINCENT PEGGY JOYCE PATSY JIM MARIAN NORMAN KIT STUART

Yours ever,

Ralph

Father's card from the P.O.W. Camp, dated 23.1.1944.

Later we understood that he did not know if we were still in South Africa or whether we had managed to return to England.

Although we were accustomed now to not having a father in our lives, I think Lindsey and I were becoming aware that our lives were rather different from most of our school friends' who, of course, had 'normal' homes and families and had South African roots, whereas we were definitely English and felt a bit out on a limb at times. Perhaps having a mother who was not very strong also contributed to this feeling, and I remember sometimes longing to have a father and even a home of our own and to be more like everyone else! Looking back, however, I realise how wonderfully Mother coped with the

It's alright now – God is in charge!

situation, feeling confident that one day we would return to England and hopefully that Father would come back to us, and how her faith in God never wavered; this has always been a real encouragement to me!

Chapter Fourteen

Red Letter Day!

Gradually there was news about the ending of the war in the Far East. We knew, of course, about the joy of VE Day in May but still longed for the war in the Far East to end too. Then we heard about a nuclear bomb – the atom bomb – and on 15th August, 1945, VJ Day, the definite ending of the War! This was formalized on board the battleship 'USS Missourie' in Tokyo Bay on 2nd September, 1945. It all seemed so amazing, unbelievable, exciting, and very difficult to take in quite what was happening, particularly because, for a time, there was still no real news from Father.

At one of our English lessons at school, the form was asked what a 'Red Letter Day' was; usually I was too shy to speak up in class, but this time I raised my hand enthusiastically and told everyone that for me a Red Letter Day would be the day my Father came back from the War! This was greeted kindly and sympathetically, even though much later I understood it was not quite the required answer!

Then – wonderfully exciting – there was an exchange of many cables between Mother and Father; they were actually managing at long last to be in touch with one another! Father was on his way to us! I am not sure when he first realised that we were still in South Africa, but he disembarked from his ship on its way to England at Port Said, Cairo. He would still have been under military discipline, but I know he happily volunteered to accompany a blind South African man to Durban. This friend had been blinded as a P.O.W. As a consequence of his offer, Father was enabled to leave his ship and then to reach us in Grahamstown by train.

It's alright now – God is in charge!

I have the postcard he sent to his mother, obviously after he had written his first letter to her. It has an attractive scene of the pyramids in Egypt. On the reverse side, with the address (it is dated 27th October, 1945, and stamped Mombasa, Kenya) he has written on it, "EX-POW MAIL" and, "AIR MAIL". There is no postage stamp; it simply says:

> My dear Mother,
>
> We reach Mombasa this afternoon, and, probably, Durban within a week. Much love to you all, especially to your dear self,
>
> > Your son,
> >
> > > Ralph

Lindsey and I also received postcards with Egyptian scenes. It was thrilling beyond words to have these; they arrived at Dorset House and were very precious. I wish I still had mine! But I do have the first letter Father wrote to Mother! It is written in pencil and then carefully folded so that part of the back was used for the address. It was addressed to The Hope (also in pencil) and re-addressed (in black ink) to Mrs Favell at Grahamstown, postmarked "3Oct45". In red ink there are the words "POW mail" and some illegible writing which looks like:

> % Recovered P. W. Taral Cambria (??)
> Bombay
> India Command
> 151

In faded pencil on a piece of now-yellowed, foolscap, lined paper Father writes:

> TAMUAN CAMP, THAILAND
>
> > 2.9.45
>
> My darling,
>
> You will have realised by now how very meagre our outward communications have been allowed to be while P.O.W.s. Similarly later have been those to us. The last card from you was dated 29.2.44 (received towards the end of '44) and I am anxiously waiting to know where you are. Your last letter was

dated 30.8.43 – the last of a series which gave a clear and delightful picture of your life. If the twins ever wrote letters or if photos or parcels were sent, they never reached me. I have no doubt that you will have heard by wireless broadcast or by a stereotyped army cable sent to The Hope that I am in Thailand still, having been here since the end of June, 1942, & on the whole I have suffered little from disease – dysentery (mild) in 1942 BT malaria and jaundice 1944 – but I have had a severe sort of 'flu for several days and am still running a temperature – a confounded nuisance at this stage!

Thanks to the devoted efforts of some very brave men we have rarely been without news for long. Wireless sets were kept going in water bottles (until the Nips spotted that one) & otherwise disguised and were smuggled from place to place with great ingenuity. Some radio operators died of the mistreatment they received when caught. This news service ceased early this year, but we have kept partly in touch through Thais and by air pamphlets. Thais have also assisted some of us to obtain funds and therefore additions to an inadequate diet. Now there is too much to eat – but how sick we are of rice!

Soon after reaching Thailand I was given a clerical job on the administration side which I have held ever since. This accounts for my comparatively good health, for although I have been right up not very far from Burma Border, I never suffered the terrible hardships inflicted on the men slaving on the railway.

Yesterday five planes showered supplies on us, it was quite a local entertainment! I hope there will be some decent baccy! It is still hard to realise that this show is over, but it is!!

I am longing for news of everyone. There are no postal facilities for us yet & I don't know how this scrawl will reach you. I am hoping soon to get the Bank's instructions where to go (if the army leaves a choice later). Meanwhile I had to say Malaya.

There are a thousand questions I want to ask and a thousand things to say – & soon! My love to the twins, bless them and you.

Ralph

P.S. Since writing the foregoing it appears I have malaria again as well! There is however a new and more effective treatment evolved in the Burma campaign so it won't take long to cure.

It's alright now – God is in charge!

> *Also postcards from the Twins written Dec 1944 arrived yesterday, but none from you. How delighted I was, but how much more I should have been to have heard also from you.*

I also have the letter he wrote to my Uncle Jim (Mother's brother) in England. Not being in his handwriting, it might have been dictated or, perhaps, copied for Mother, and is rather illegible in parts. I quote:

> *No 2 Group*
> *Camp Tamuan*
> *Thailand*
>
> *30/8/45*

My dear Jim,

You will have realised by now that our outward communications while POW (indecipherable word) if they went, were restricted to one miserable postcard of the field type, about twice or three times a year and possibly a telegram once so that I have had no opportunity of thanking you before for your letter written two years and one week ago from an address most carefully obliterated by the Censor. This letter only reached me a few months ago.

The position here is strange. Although we have just taken over the guard, the Japs are not completely disarmed owing to the danger to them from local inhabitants; we are not armed at all but two parachutists who have come in with wireless are! Evacuation by air to Rangoon has begun but not yet for us. American parachutists have been arming and training Thais for the last three months in the jungle about 30 miles away and have been keen to get American and other POWs to join them. This was discouraged by our authorities because so few POWs were in any condition to be of use for long, and because the Japs had unpleasant methods of dealing with the camp from which there were many escapes and this was very largely a base hospital.

We have never been without news of the war for very long, even in the remote jungle. Amazing receivers were constructed; some in water bottles – a trick to which the Japs eventually got wise, but the most successful of our operators succeeded this year in getting parts of their sets inserted into a Japanese officer's water-bottle when they were sent to Bangkok and he unwittingly took it for them. At considerable risks Thais have passed news and papers in, and Air Force pamphlets have been smuggled in. Some wireless men have been so badly beaten and mistreated that they have died.

For that matter, apart from the mass murder of sending men into these jungles without proper food or accommodation and with inadequate drugs, and weakened as they were by privations, forcing them to labour from before dawn till after dark, and to live without shelter in monsoon conditions, men have been murdered by blows because they were too weak and too ill (even to lie on stretchers, in which they were carried from camps), to break stones.

My party came to Thailand at the end of June 1942 from Singapore, road making during July, and in August I was given a clerical job in the administration. This turned out to be keeping records of individuals who joined the group (No 2 POW Thailand) so that mail could be distributed (the first letters came in 1943) and later keeping records of deaths, so that, although I have been nearly as far as the Burma border, I escaped the worst hardships of the railway. Also, apart from a mild go of dysentery in October – November 1942, B.T., malaria Feb – June 1944 and the odd dengue fever, my health has been comparatively good. At the present I am laid up with fever (flu'?) which is prevalent and is some excuse for this awful scrawl.

I have not said how much I appreciated your letter. My love to Sally (Jim's wife) and the children. Congrats to Brendan on his scholarship. I trust you are well, dear man. I have not had a card from Sheila since one dated February 1944, so that I do not know where she is; also I have no idea where the Bank wish me to go. It is still quite hard to realise that this life is nearly over. All the best to you all.

Ralph

2.9.45 Have had a lousy temperature since I wrote, which has gone this morning, I hope for good.

It's alright now – God is in charge!

Besides writing to Mother and several others, Father also wrote to Penny, my aunt. I have her letter, written in pencil, and I quote this too:

Bangkok

12/9/45

My Dearest Penny,

You will now know that the Japs would only permit the most meagre of outward, and later inward, communications, so that I was never able to reply to your letters; but how I thank you for them! I had been somewhat anxious, driving an air raid ambulance was apt to be dangerous (Penny had served with the Voluntary Ambulance Drivers) and I was delighted to read of your renewed gardening enterprise. Thank goodness you came through.

The European internees organised 'underground' supplies of funds and such medicines as they could attain, and both they and their Chinese and Thai conspirators deserve the highest praise for dangerous efforts. The Nips allowed the Red Cross to purchase some comforts and clothing in Thailand, but it seems they swiped our parcels, for in my POW 'Group' we only received 1/6th of one parcel each. Worse than that they withheld medical supplies.

For my own part I have been very lucky in health with much less malaria than most and only a mild go of dysentery, and having a clerical job, but the majority of other ranks have suffered terribly at times; in my group 1 in 4 ½ British officers died in Thailand, the health of many must be permanently affected and 755 men and 6 officers are missing from ships attacked while en route to Japan, so that the total British officers losses in my group are probably about 35% – 1960 out of 5569 [illegible] – and the British officers 30 out of 501 or about 6%. The underlined figures are in estimate of the average number of the British in the group and include the dead in order to ensure against exaggeration. These figures tell their own story and I won't harrow you with atrocities – you will read about them elsewhere.

Amongst the most entertaining stories you will hear will be the method by which a few very brave men kept wireless sets in operation, and how they smuggled the parts through searches from camp to camp, so that, most of the time, we had some idea of news. In fact I think we were better informed than the Nips!

The odds against escape (from the group I was in) were impossible and no one succeeded in getting through. They were all imprisoned or shot.

My present plan is to stay here, if possible, until I learn whether Sheila is still at the Cape. Once at Rangoon I might get swept out on the wrong track. A few days ago I had postcards from the twins – their first. These were dated December 1944 but the last card I have had from Sheila was dated February 1944.

I have written to Jim – and of course to Sheila and my mother, but in case my letters don't get through, will you tell them the position?

My very best love to you Penny dear, and please give my regards to the Oakleys, to the de Clairs, if you see them. Also to Dan [?] who I hope is going strong.

I am also writing to Bertha and Kit and I hope my letters will all get through.

Cheerio!

Ralph

So we began to hear the definite news of Father's return to us! Mother had sent cables with great joy, and eventually we had the wonderful news that he really was on his way to us in Grahamstown; we now had a date in November!

Our friends in Stones Hill were so marvellous to us with our returning hero. They made sure that he would know how welcome he was, offering us the use of a delightful house and being incredibly wonderful!

The Red Letter Day arrived at last! The three of us were at Grahamstown in very good time, waiting eagerly for Father! The train puffed in with much noise and steam, the many doors flew open and crowds of people erupted. We stood with our eyes watching everything and everyone, with such joyous expectation tinged with a little nervousness – what would Father look like; what would he *be* like?

Then I saw such a tall, gaunt-looking man, his face rather yellow, the thinnest person I ever remembered seeing to the point of being skeletal. But there he was – Father – striding towards us, knowing us at once, arms outstretched to us all! It was wonderful, astonishing, amazing, and very hard to take in that this was really happening! We all spoke at once; there was so much to catch up on! We happily drove up to Stones Hill, to the house that had been so kindly offered to us for this occasion, and found to our surprise that a great bed-linen sheet with the words "Welcome to Ralph" painted on it was strung across the road! How overwhelming for Father and, indeed, for all of us, and so heart-warming!

As we settled into this large and sumptuous house, feeling a little awed by it all, I asked Father how he had recognized us; he said, with a twinkle in his eye, that he had inquired everywhere he went what eleven-year-old girls would look like so he knew us at once!

It was hard to know where to begin to try to catch up with each other; in fact this seemed impossible! Lindsey and I were to be with our parents for the whole weekend, returning to Dorset House afterwards, so this was a very precious time. However, we found it was surprisingly difficult to get to know Father again, and it was actually a very disillusioning experience. He was so different and, of course, I realised afterwards, he was still traumatized by the terrible ordeals he had suffered as a P.O.W. under the Japanese. He found that an ordinary bed was not a good idea; he just couldn't sleep with such 'cushiness' and managed to find a camp bed in the house, which suited him much better. He found that mealtimes were difficult too and often said he wasn't hungry, so didn't join us, and he seemed to need to be on his own quite a lot. He had brought his 'billy-can'[32] with him, something that perhaps he had had to keep with him always. It was rather battered and dented and certainly made quite an impression on me. I know he suffered terrible nightmares, and although he simply loved being with his family again, it was a huge adjustment, which I don't think any of us had been able to foresee.

Lindsey and I duly returned to school, and I remember trying hard not to feel so disappointed and sad, and rather guilty, that it was actually a relief to return to the more 'normal life' to which I was accustomed to by then. Mother told me years afterwards that it was a very painful time for her too; naturally he wanted to talk about quite

---

[32] or 'mess-tin'

a lot of what had happened, although I do not think he ever went into too many of the harrowing details; Mother was very shocked by some of the stories and just could not relate to them at all.

No one then really knew the extent of the appalling treatment these P.O.W.s had endured, and it was extremely hard to take it all in. Some men even had to sign a paper that they would *not* tell of their experiences because USA and Britain wanted to get back to important trade with Japan – but I do not know if Father had to sign such a document. Nobody in those days had counselling, and many people thought it best if these traumatized people said very little about their experiences and just put it all behind them. It is very different these days!

Father had had the most amazing answers to prayer and started a quest to know God more. While in Grahamstown he sought the Dean of the Cathedral in order to have confirmation classes and found this to be a real help; I was very impressed by this and longed to join a class too!

The dear Tarka Bridge community had been so faithful in daily prayer for Father all those years as, indeed, had his whole family. It was truly wonderful to hear that when he had been in great pain with a dreadful back condition and, like everyone else, had been expected to continue to do the impossibly hard labour on the Siam/Burma railway, the Japanese officer commanding the work force on a particular day had ordered him to do clerical work instead, much to his astonishment! Later, this officer told him that he had recognized him from working under him in the Hong Kong and Shanghai Bank in Kobe, that he had remembered Father being kind to him and so had spared him that really hard labour, clerical duties being totally different! How we praise God for this!

Another time, when suffering from beri-beri, a rare Red Cross parcel had been delivered to his group. The Red Cross were marvellous in sending aid, but this hardly ever reached the men for whom it was intended, the Japanese taking nearly everything. He had been given a small jar of Marmite, which he had promptly shared with another suffering P.O.W., and this was just the very thing needed to counteract the horrible disease, Vitamin B being the perfect medication! I believe this worked wonders for both these men!

It's alright now – God is in charge!

My sister told me how once, many years later, she went with Father to visit an ex-P.O.W friend, and this man told her how generous Father had been to others in the camps whenever it was possible. We loved hearing these things about him!

Father did talk about some of the good things in his P.O.W. experiences, his friends and comrades and, particularly, his great admiration for the news bulletins obtained at the risk of the death penalty. Also he spoke of how much he admired the Thai people who had courageously done what they could for the P.O.W.s. Father must have had a role in these secrets because he would tell gleefully of the different ruses that people managed and was full of admiration for the skill of the technicians. I realise that much courage was shown in the determination to hear the latest news for everyone, even at such risk – and several of these brave men were tortured and killed.

He spoke too about the beauty of the river and the boats with friendly Thai people, and how he had enjoyed the entertainments later on, the pleasure of making a chess set and playing this game with friends by the light of the moon.

But, all the same, the ghastly conditions and the atrocious behaviour of the Japanese to their Prisoners of War certainly took their toll; perhaps none of us will ever be able to really understand how terrible it all was for all these men. I have read many books written by P.O.W.s and realise that their war was awful beyond words. So it really was not surprising, with all we now know, how difficult it must have been for Father and all the other survivors to come to terms with what had happened in these past years and to be able to relate easily again with their families. But it was marvellous that he had survived, and we were more grateful for this than we ever could express!

One of the more difficult things Mother found was that Father could not relate to her experiences either, and he seemed to have little understanding about what she had gone through in these last years! I wonder, a bit, if that was because in the light of what he had suffered, her ordeals seemed so very much less. I think she would have loved to have been able to share some of the troubles of being on her own in a strange country, without her husband and not knowing what was happening to him or even if she would ever see him again. The financial situation was not easy either; she did receive a regular income from the Hong Kong and Shanghai Bank but believed she should live on as little as possible in order to try to save as much as possible for him should they ever be reunited.

Father did not understand us either; he had missed so much of our childhood, and it may have been a shock to him to find out about our inadequate schooling, the lack of sport in our lives, our great love for horses and life on a farm!

Father had quite a lot of mood swings, again difficult to cope with, and sometimes he seemed very unreasonable. Mother tried her best to help in every way she could. They truly loved one another, and their love certainly saw them through this traumatic time.

When we returned from school, on holiday this time, we all went to The Hope. Everyone there was so looking forward to meeting him, and he then saw something of our life and the lovely people who meant so much to us. I am sure there must have been great prayers of thanksgiving for his return to us all! But, there was a new situation for Lindsey and me; Mother had been the one in authority all those years, and I found it strangely difficult when Father asserted his role as father! There were little things... For example, he was really shocked that all of us children usually went barefoot; we hardly ever wore shoes! No doubt having experienced some of the horrors of having no shoes on the 'death railway', he anxiously warned of dire consequences, of diseases we could pick up, not to mention painful thorns and other horrors! And then, much to my dismay, for the very first time, Lindsey *did* have a thorn in her foot, and he insisted that she went to the hospital in Cradock to have it removed! We were not allowed to go barefoot again! He was most uneasy when we happily ate guavas, which have little seeds in them, and also any bananas which were black at one end. I remember being amazed at all this 'pettiness' and finding I felt very rebellious! There were several other things, and I realised I much preferred the way Mother had been our 'authority' but felt very torn because I actually wanted to look up to Father admiringly!

I think we may have been a disappointment to him too; he had been such a sportsman, and it must have been sadly obvious that neither of us were! I remember him commenting on the way one of our friends could run so well and suggesting that we copied her example, and how I felt it seemed that I just wasn't up to his standard in anything. But I also remember looking at him with my whole attention trying to take a photo of him in my mind, particularly on one occasion, when he came out of the sitting room through the fly-proof door onto the stoep in the Favell's house and bent down to tap his pipe on his shoe to empty it, and how he carefully filled the bowl with tobacco, stuffing it in firmly, and then lit it, drawing in the smoke and puffing it out happily! It was a dear and familiar procedure, and I suddenly knew, with great clarity, that I loved my Father dearly!

Our parents shortly before being parted again

After he had been with us for four months Father heard that he was to return to the Hong Kong and Shanghai Bank for work again and that his next post would be first in Peking and then in Tientsin, China! There was no shipping to speak of, as many ships had been lost in the war; there were no passages possible for his wife and children, so he had to go to China leaving us and departing on his own again. This must have been very hard for both parents, but the Hong Kong and Shanghai Bank urgently needed to get their offices working properly as soon as possible, and my parents seemed to accept the situation with amazing forbearance; this was, in fact, how life in the bank had always been. I know now that Father was nowhere near ready to return to work, particularly on his own.

He sent us attractive postcards from Shanghai, which I still have. He wrote telling us about Peking and the wonder and interest of it all, and also how much he was missing us. We learnt through his letters that Tientsin was bitterly cold that winter – a 'five-coat' winter, because that was how many padded coats the Chinese people needed to wear to try to keep warm! But the house he was allocated in Tientsin did not have anything near adequate heating, and he was seriously cold, especially after the heat of the tropics.

Mother's faith must have been painfully tested. She longed to return to England and then to be able to join her husband, but first she knew she would have to find the right school for her daughters, and it still seemed impossible to get a passage back to the UK. My deep impression of her always was that she serenely put her trust in her loving God and waited to see how prayers would be answered.

In the meanwhile, another of my prayers was answered: Lindsey and I were able to join a confirmation class at school with the Dean of Grahamstown Cathedral. I was thrilled! I loved being able to hear about the 'important things that really mattered', and I knew all over again that our God really does answer prayer! I realised we may have to wait to be confirmed on our return to England; but so much was happening with another new challenging stage ahead, I was certain that confirmation would take its place at the right time later.

Eventually Mother managed to find a passage for us on the 'Caernarvon Castle', Union Castle Line, sailing from Cape Town in November, 1946, and suddenly we had the pleasure of buying new clothes for our new life in England. It seemed a whole new beginning was ahead of us again. Mother, Lindsey and I were able to look back over the years in South Africa, reminding each other of the way God had taken care of us all, how he had brought Father back to us and had answered every prayer in his wonderful way and timing. I am still very thankful!

CHAPTER FIFTEEN

Father's War

*F*ather had suffered greatly as a prisoner of war under the Imperial Japanese Army in Malaya. As a member of the Settlement Volunteers he had taken part in the defence of Singapore and was wounded, the scars from a bullet wound passing through his left shoulder blade from front to back still being evident many years later. However, he was very relieved that his wife and family had escaped safely before Singapore surrendered to the Japanese Army, who were the vastly superior force at the time. Although he knew they had disembarked from their ship, SS Colborne, at Cape Town, he hoped that they would then have been able to return safely to England.

To give a little of the background about Japan at the time of WWII, I will explain simply some of the history; I believe we need to understand the circumstances of that era and something more about the Japanese culture and their outlook on life.

The culture and traditions of Japan go back at least ten thousand years; the Japanese were a gifted and creative people with beautiful artwork and charming manners and customs. But their ideology is very different from the Western philosophy, and with a mutual lack of understanding between the cultures each would be horrified at the other's ideas! For example, surrender was unthinkable to the Japanese while their seemingly casual attitude to life was appalling to the Western mind.

There was a varied assortment of different Shinto and Buddhist sects, all combining to form a spiritual framework for the Japanese.

136

There must be over a hundred thousand Shinto shrines all over Japan, and these are the most sacred spaces in the land. Shinto became the state religion and was used to promote a distinct ideology of Japanese superiority. They believed that they were a superior race because of their divine origins; these ideas were taught in schools and in all public life. They despised all other races, especially the Chinese whom they regarded as particularly inferior.[33]

Until they suffered crushing defeat at the hands of the US in WWII, Japanese religion focused around the figure of the Emperor, who was considered a living god and whose subjects saw themselves as part of a huge family in which all Japanese people were members. The defeat, however, shattered many people's beliefs, as the frail voice of the Emperor was broadcast in 1946 in an address called the 'Declaration of Humanity', renouncing his deity and, at the same time, also denouncing the racial superiority of Japanese people.

Here are some notes that my husband Hugh wrote some time ago:

July 1940: The Japanese Government resigned and was replaced by one of complete control of expansionist and militant elements. Japan had demanded that Britain close the Burma Road (Rangoon to Chungking, in China) along which military supplies were reaching China. Most supplies were from USA, but USA would not give any assurance of support if Britain refused Japan's demand. Britain consequently closed the Burma Road on 18th July.

23rd September, 1940: Japan occupied Indo China which was under Vichy French control.

29th September, 1940: Japan signed Tripartite Pact with Germany and Italy.

16th October, 1940: USA put control on export of steel and iron scrap on which Japan had been dependent.

April 1941: Japan and Russia signed Neutrality Pact.

---

[33] There seems to be a likeness to the German ideology under Hitler over Jewish people.

It's alright now – God is in charge!

> *22nd June, 1941:* Germany invaded Russia.[34]

> *21st July, 1941: Vichy French Government submitted to Japan's demands to occupy Indo China. By the end of July Japan had occupied the whole of South Indo China.*

> *26th-28th July, 1941: The USA, the British and the Dutch froze all Japanese assets and existing trade treaties with Japan, thus stopping all trade between these countries and Japan. This meant cutting off all supplies of materials useful in war, such as oil from Dutch East Indies.*

> *31st July, 1941: A message from Tokyo to the Japanese Ambassador in Berlin was intercepted and decoded in which was said that the economic position resulting from these actions taken by the USA, Great Britain and the Netherlands would become so serious that it could not be endured for long.*

The Japanese were seeking to enlarge their territories, being worryingly short of raw materials for their growing industries and increasing population; a peaceful solution was not an option. The West had many colonies; Japan was late on the scene.

The Japanese had first invaded China in 1931, and in the major attack of 1937-1938 they overran most of northern and central China, capturing Peking in July 1937 and causing havoc and terror with their unspeakable cruelties. They then worked their way southwards. With an eye on the strategic positions of Hong Kong and Singapore, they were also determined to conquer the Dutch East Indies and every Pacific island with oil deposits and useful resources; they were incredibly ruthless, desperate to achieve their objectives.

Recently it has come to light that there were British secret agents working for the Japanese who gave much needed assistance in revealing how to achieve some of their aims, even to the extent of revealing the best designs in aircraft, warships and effective methods of modern warfare. This treacherous help did much to enable the fall of Singapore; some historians say that without this aid there would not have been an invasion and Singapore would not have had to

---

[34] One effect of Germany's invasion of Russia was that Russia became Britain's ally. Russia then required military equipment from Britain, for which the Royal Navy had the additional burden of resources to protect supplies by the sea route to Archangel.

surrender. Spies were established everywhere in the Far East, particularly in Malaya, many years beforehand, taking hundreds of photos and discovering, amongst other details, all possible routes away from the main roads. Later these country roads were essential for the invasion and particularly important for the troops on bicycles.

From childhood almost every man in Japan had trained for war, so the army, navy and air force were well prepared for battles. The armed forces were obedient and answerable to Emperor Hirohito only. Their large fleets of aircraft and ships were ready for war as soon as the signals were given. There were 'peace talks' and meetings with world leaders, particularly the USA, but even while negotiations were taking place there was no intention of actually complying.

On Christmas Day 1941, Hong Kong (not able to be fully prepared) was captured after brief and very fierce battles, with a huge number of casualties and deaths.[35] But it seemed that Singapore was amazingly complacent as people there felt that Singapore was impregnable; after all, weren't the coastal guns all firmly pointing out to sea? If there was to be an invasion surely the Japanese would attack from the sea! These guns would have been very useful had they had the correct ammunition when the actual battle for Singapore took place as, in fact, they could be aimed anywhere! It was only when Pearl Harbour was attacked on 7/8th December, 1941 that America declared war. Since about January 1941 Japan had been secretly planning to attack Pearl Harbour where so much of the USA Fleet were stationed, vulnerable and at their mercy.

Two British battleships had just been sent to give Singapore a boost to the defences, but the few Brewster Buffalo aircraft provided were woefully inadequate as the war in Europe against the German Army still needed all the armaments possible. The battleships, 'Repulse' and the 'Prince of Wales' were deployed at once after war on Japan was declared and, appallingly, were both sunk by pouncing Japanese bombers off the coast of north Malaya. There are some wonderful stories of the courage of the men who survived and of the many who were drowning; it has been very inspiring to learn about this.

---

[35] Hugh's parents were in Hong Kong at the time and were taken prisoner along with hundreds of other civilians who all suffered terribly.

Apparently it was not expected that the Japanese Army would invade Malaya from the North, but they came in their thousands in every form of vehicle, from bicycles to tanks, brutally killing civilians and mercilessly proceeding southwards. The British and Australian forces (many of who were not fully trained or acclimatised, and were by then extremely weary) were forced to retreat the whole way to Singapore. Japanese bombers attacked all the major towns, and suddenly peaceful, beautiful Malaya became a terrible warzone with hundreds of innocent people being brutalized and cruelly punished, while others were taken prisoner, often in appalling conditions.

After approximately a week of fierce fighting, Singapore surrendered. There were many terrible problems for the Allied Army, not least the impending, serious shortage of water as well as military supplies, food and petrol. With the massive casualties, it was a difficult but necessary decision. The Singapore surrender was considered to be one of the most tragic defeats of WWII. The Japanese then raised their 'Rising Sun' flag triumphantly on the tallest building standing in Singapore, and the defeated army was marched as prisoners of war to the barracks at Changi to begin many years of dreadful suffering.

Father said very little about his experiences as a P.O.W. and seemed to make light of his ordeals. It was almost impossible for these men to even try to begin to tell what they had gone through. Civilians simply could not comprehend the dreadful and unheard of atrocities in their treatment by their captors. I found the Japanese mentality easier to understand when I knew that the Japanese would commit suicide rather than surrender and that they deeply despised those who did surrender, regarding themselves as the supreme race, all others being inferior to them and not even worthy of their consideration.

The Japanese Army then had an unforeseen problem to cope with at the fall of Singapore: what were they to do with these thousands of prisoners, army personnel and civilians? How were they to be fed; where would they be housed?

Immediately they made it clear that they were the victors by their intimidating behaviour and, as previously in Hong Kong, they were vicious in their punishments and tortures from the beginning. Amongst other acts, they raped the nurses in the hospitals. They used the wounded lying in their hospital beds for cold-blooded bayonet practice. With all the killing and maiming in Malaya they continued to be as terrifying as they had been the whole way from China southwards. No wonder they had such a terrible reputation! They had been trained from childhood to be ruthless and were a remarkably well-disciplined army, rigidly obedient to their Emperor God. They were brought up believing that death in battle was the only alternative to victory. Such was their discipline that even the Japanese soldiers were severely punished if they did not completely conform to any orders.

So much has now been written about the ghastly happenings from the start of this successful Japanese invasion of Malaya: the forced marches under extreme conditions; the often unnecessary and deliberate deprivation of food, water and medicines; the demand for respect to the Japanese guards with the prisoners always having to bow to them[36]; the beatings for the least infringement of petty rules; the outright and often sadistic torture; and inhumane behaviour at every level. These horrendous times seemed to bring out the very best or the very worst in people. The overcrowded conditions for both P.O.W.s and civilians, the increasing starvation and the lack of medical supplies made life intolerable, yet there are many inspiring stories of how wonderfully some people rose above these situations, becoming outstanding heroes and encouraging others.

I imagine Father, being wounded, was still forced to march to Changi Barracks where the P.O.W.s were to be incarcerated. Many local people lined the route, offering food and water with kind sympathy, and this was very much appreciated! These Malay, Chinese or Indian people would also suffer dreadfully, and many thousands perished during the years to come.

The Japanese were planning to build a new railway from Thailand to Burma for the transport of war materials and supplies. They wanted to create a new overland route from Rangoon to the Bay of Bengal and through Bangkok to Singapore, preferring this to using the Allied-controlled seas with their submarines and aircraft.

They also had their eyes on the British Empire in India. Having surveyed the incredibly difficult terrain with its steep valleys and hills

---

[36] Westerners did not realise this is an important part of their culture!

it was realised that a vast number of workers would be required to achieve this ambitious project. The height difference along this railway would be around three hundred meters and include viaducts and bridges. The estimated time to build the new rail link was about five to six years, but now it was to be completed within as short a time as possible – urgently! The P.O.W.s would make an excellent work force – slave labour in abundance!

The men in their thousands were taken northwards from Singapore by train in what sounded like horrendous conditions. The metal railway wagons were greatly overcrowded and became like ovens in the tropical heat, with no windows, fresh air or light. Many of the P.O.W.s were suffering from dysentery; not everyone was able to sit, let alone lie down, and many men died.

When, after about five days of that horrific journey, the exhausted men arrived at their destination, they found they had to march to their first 'camp' for a great many kilometres. Any stragglers were beaten, or bayonetted, or even just left to die, with no mercy shown whatsoever. On arrival at their destination it was only to discover that in fact this 'camp' was not prepared for them. The prisoners then had to start building their huts, using timber, bamboo and all they could find from the engulfing jungle to make these essential shelters. These were very basic and did not offer enough protection from heavy tropical rains, especially in the monsoon seasons. All the while they would be screamed at by the Japanese to hurry; "Speedo, speedo!" was the ceaseless command heard during the next years.

Most of these P.O.W.s were probably not used to the jungle, while the Japanese had had some considerable training in such areas. Struggling to find routes through the dense undergrowth was always incredibly difficult, with sharp thorns tearing flesh, feet and clothes. All the work done on the railway had to be done by hand with the most basic of implements. There certainly wasn't any earth-moving equipment, although at times elephants were used to move the heaviest logs and timbers cut from the surrounding jungle. The humid, oppressive heat, was often overwhelming, the strong odours of decay sometimes revolting, and many species of insects would have attacked these people relentlessly. There were so many unfamiliar and horrible things to cope with, never enough water or food and always the thought of a sudden and unprovoked beating from an angry guard.

As time went on relentlessly, their clothes wore out, and the men were often reduced to making loincloths out of whatever material they could find. Footwear became a major problem, and terrible foot injuries were a consequence of the lack of protection. Painful leg ulcers became the norm, but starvation also took its toll, the lack of medication and vitamins so often causing unnecessary hardship. Dreadful diseases such as malaria, beri-beri, dysentery, and cholera swept through the camps, with dire results; thousands died, and to avoid further deaths and the spread of diseases, particularly cholera, bodies were collected and cremated in huge piles, sometimes even before they had quite died.

The men were reduced to skeletons, exhausted and ill and yet still forced to work: heaving heavy timbers, blasting rock in order to create passes through the often steep mountain sides, and building viaducts high above the river along which the new railway was being created. These tall structures were mostly made from bamboo, a very strong material, the men having to climb precarious-looking scaffolding to build them with no protection whatever. And all this to the shouts and screams of the Japanese who seemed to become yet more brutal and demanding as the deadline to have the railway completed drew nearer. The famished men worked sixteen hours in the tropical heat, day after day, with no respite and in appalling conditions.

The punishments meted out to people for the least offences were very cruel, in addition to the savage beatings. These would include being made to kneel on sharp sticks while holding a heavy boulder for several hours at a time, being tied to a tree with barbed wire and left for two or three days without food or water; sometimes there would be a container of water put just out of reach of the poor victim. There was also the 'water treatment' when the prisoner would be forced to drink a large quantity of water with the torturers then jumping onto his extended stomach. It is sad to say that the Japanese seemed to enjoy this kind of entertainment.

One of the most dreaded punishments was the Black Hole, when a bamboo cage was created just below ground, too small for anyone to stretch out or ease his limbs in, with a corrugated iron cover fixed firmly on top of this. The victim would be left for several days, again without food or water, in what must have been an oven in the hot sun, suffering immeasurably in complete darkness with the appalling stench also from previous prisoners' faeces, and sometimes causing them to roast slowly to death.

It must also have been very hard for the other prisoners to witness these tortures and know that they could do nothing to help. Some of the memories of their comrades sufferings would linger on for years to come: hearing their screams of pain, or just seeing the silent courage of many who were in agony and dying.

The army doctors in the camps did their best to alleviate as much distress as possible, and having few resources they improvised in many amazing ways. Amputation was often the only answer to excruciatingly painful leg ulcers, involving surgery without anaesthetics, and then there would be great problems over keeping wounds free from infection. But there are many stories of how the men survived, recovered and were enabled to walk again with the aid of improvised crutches and even new 'limbs' fashioned cleverly from bamboo and other materials. One of the 'prescriptions' was to get maggots to clean wounds. It sounds awful, but these creatures would eat the rotten flesh away and actually did a good job! It was evident from the extensive and deep scars on his legs that Father had also suffered leg ulcers, but I do not know whether maggots were used in his case.

Construction of the Burma 'death railway' began in October 1942, and with all the forced labour was first put into use on 25th October, 1943, quite amazing when the first estimate was that it would take about five years to build! The railway was about 260 miles long, 188 miles of which was in Thailand and 68 miles in Burma. The line, begun at either end, met somewhere near the 'Three Pagoda Pass'. But the notorious 'Hellfire Pass', reached in June 1943, had to be undertaken first, an incredibly difficult area to first blast a way through and then to build a huge viaduct under horrendous conditions. Sixty-eight men were beaten to death at this point. It was appalling that many thousands of prisoners died – it has been said 'one life for every railway sleeper', making us appreciate Father's survival all the more.

The dreadful 1943 monsoon caused much havoc. Father's hut, housing a great many men, collapsed. He described the ensuing mess as terrible, with deep slimy mud, no doubt stinking with the latrines overflow. He then described having to build another hut in those conditions as most unpleasant. After that awful monsoon the number of P.O.W.s was so depleted that the Japanese ordered that some two hundred thousand Asian labourers were to be employed. These were civilians who were told that they could take paid work in the country, with good conditions, and because life was very hard at that time in Malaya thousands accepted this enticing offer. Many of these men suffered even more than the Allied P.O.W.s due to the fact that they did not have the background army discipline, medical aid or any organisational skills. Because of serious malnutrition and encountering horrendous diseases, very tragically, about one hundred and fifty thousand of these workers died.

When the railway was completed, thirty thousand men were kept in a few camps to maintain it, and the pressure eased for the P.O.W.s; gradually, even though they were all emaciated and weak, they began to think of entertainments, amazingly producing plays and even improvising some instruments for concerts. Everyone had an opportunity to take part, perhaps making posters, background scenery or costumes as well. The Japanese officers also enjoyed these performance times and would make sure they always had the best front 'seats'!

There were several men with great talents for drawing, painting with cleverly made colours to depict clearly some of the horrors of the camps. These were carefully hidden in bamboo and, amazingly, some were retrieved later, giving us an inkling of the appalling conditions of being P.O.W.s under the Japanese Army.

Father was musical and would remember beautiful pieces from his youth, replaying them in his head, and found this so helpful, even consoling very often when in distress. Father made himself a chess set from bamboo and later replaced this with one he was able to buy; this set he gave to his first great-grandchild, Jonathan Buckwell. There is a typed note in the attractive box in which he kept it.

Ralph Wallace Lee's note from the chess set he gave to his first great-grandchild, Jonathan Buckwell.

This set fits into a round 50 cigarette tin. I bought it in a camp not far from 3 Pagoda Pass (Siam-Burmah border) after the 1943 monsoon when cholera was rife. It replaced one I'd made from bamboo and I counted it after every use – conditions were pretty rough. In the drier weather chess became very popular when possible – the tropical moon sometimes gave enough light. Well, it survived after travelling far and is still intact.

Father's precious chess set is kept in the decorative Chinese box, now belonging to Jonathan. The note reads: "This set fits into a round 50 cigarette tin. I bought it in a camp not far from the 3 Pagoda Pass (Siam-Burma border) after the 1943 monsoon when cholera was rife. It replaced one I'd made from bamboo and I counted it after every use – conditions were pretty rough. In the drier weather chess became very popular when possible – the tropical moon sometimes gave enough light. Well, it survived after travelling far and is still intact."

There were some wonderful padres who would hold worship services; this had a great influence on many of the prisoners, and I believe this included my Father. I remember him telling how instead of bread and wine, rice and water were used at Holy Communion services, and these symbolic elements were of great importance at the time.

One of the things that I have found so inspiring was the courageous determination of these men to make the most of every situation, finding ways to cope with unbelievable horrors through their resourcefulness and an astonishing continuing sense of humour, which must have been essential. Another marvellous fact is how the Thais tried to help the P.O.W.s as much as possible and what a huge difference this made too; they were so brave in their efforts and were greatly appreciated.

When the Japanese began to send trains full of troops and supplies to Burma, the Allies started bombing the railway, causing many deaths, not realising that our P.O.W.s were in the vicinity. A cause of unnecessary danger to the men was that they were not permitted to make the symbol of a P.O.W. camp for the bombers (a white triangle on a blue background) or even allowed to dig trenches to protect themselves – until many were killed. So with the continued bombing endless repairs were essential, particularly for the bridges.

A Secret Imperial Order, in 1944, was given to every Japanese camp throughout Asia to prepare for the execution of all their P.O.W.s as soon as the Allies started to invade their conquered territories or Japan itself; the order, then, was to be definitely carried out in September 1945. To this end many prisoners were forced to dig trenches around each camp in preparation for the murders and the necessary mass graves.

However, the Allies had given an ultimatum to the Japanese to surrender on 28th July, 1945, and when this was ignored the atomic bombs were dropped first on Hiroshima, on 6th August, and then, with still no response from the Japanese, on Nagasaki, on the 9th August, thus ending this brutal war, with the Japanese finally surrendering on 15th August, 1945.

These atom bombs were devastating in every way. Many thousands of people were killed, with thousands more suffering from the then unknown dreadful effects of radiation. It has been estimated, however, that without the bombs there would have been far greater numbers of people killed. All the remaining P.O.W.s would have been executed, the Japanese army would have committed suicide (and possibly many civilians also), and the whole country would have suffered the terrible consequences.

Apparently Japan has denied everything about their part in WWII. They have rewritten their history and school books in an effort to falsely show that they were the victims of the War, citing the atomic bombs as proof of their victimization. But truth cannot be hidden, and it is best to be honest about all such things, acknowledging faults on both sides and seeking forgiveness and true reconciliation.

There are some inspirational stories told of how individuals did forgive the Japanese for the horrors they had suffered and witnessed. I am particularly awed by Bishop Leonard Wilson's story of forgiveness after appalling torture. He was the Bishop of Singapore at that time and was falsely accused of spying. When praying that he would find it possible to forgive, he was enabled to see how his oppressors (with their cruel sadistic expressions, taking it in turns to beat and torture him, with some of them actually enjoying this) would have been as little children. "You cannot hate a small child." Furthermore, he saw them as how they could alter, being redeemed by the power of Jesus Christ, "their cruelty becoming kindness, their sadistic instincts changed to gentleness". So, with God's help, he did forgive them! I believe this testimony made a deep impression on Father when we met the Bishop and his family on holiday, years later!

The Bishop's daughter, Susan, whom we also met sailing on that holiday and who later became ordained, tells how she was in a meeting between Christians from both sides of the Japanese war, how they each acknowledged their faults and were wonderfully forgiven and reconciled. In her talk she said that she and her family wanted "to affirm that unconditional forgiveness, true reconciliation can only happen when there is an acknowledgement of wrongs done, when the truth is faced and painful self-examination leads to confession and apology". It was great to hear that; real forgiveness is achievable, even over such terrible circumstances – and that is most encouraging to know!

CHAPTER SIXTEEN

Return to England

*I*t was exciting and yet sad, making plans for our return to England in November 1946, after six years away. We were very sorry to have to leave friends, realising we would probably not be able to see them again, but it was wonderful to know that we would soon be with Penny, and many of our other dear relations too. We were to sail from Cape Town, first travelling by train from Grahamstown.

We had one scary moment en route. The train had stopped at a station. Mother spotted a little shop on the platform, and asking us to keep an eye on the luggage, she hurried out to make her purchase. To our horror, the train suddenly started to pull out of the station and seemed to be picking up speed. My reaction was shock and a quick prayer, in a flash instantly thinking that Mother would have to catch the next train; that I did not know how soon that would be; that Mother had the tickets and passports and knew which hotel we were booked into to stay in Cape Town; and that we were utterly dependent on her! Then, to our huge relief, the train gently reversed back to the platform; Mother rapidly boarded with her purchase, and we were gratefully reunited. Do trains often behave that way, I wondered, because we would have liked some warning!

Cape Town was a great experience; and it was exhilarating to be near the enormous shops – and to discover escalators for the first time. These proved a challenge; it was hard work – and such fun – trying to climb up the 'down escalator'! We were reprimanded by Mother and, I think, several other disapproving folk too, which seemed a shame! However, it was soon time to board the ship; she had an attractively painted, lavender-coloured hull and a red funnel, I noticed, as we approached the quay. We were shown to our 'cabin'; the Caernarvon Castle was still fitted out as a troop ship, and while it was wonderful that we were able at last to get a passage, I do not think any of us anticipated sharing this vast area with perhaps about eighty others! The bunks were arranged in tight rows of three tiers each; the two lower ones were for us passengers and the top one for cabin luggage. I wonder how many passengers there were altogether...

RMS Caernarvon Castle of the Union Castle Line

The spelling of the ship's name seems to vary; it was sometimes with an 'e' and at other times without one.

She was built at the same dockyard (Harland and Wolff, Belfast) as the famous Titanic, but about fourteen years later, in 1926. She was about six hundred and thirty feet and her tonnage was 20,063. She was the first Union Castle Line motor ship.

The crew would have consisted of three hundred and fifty members, and there would normally have been some eight hundred and fifty passengers split fairly evenly between the three classes: first, second, third.

In 1938 she was modernized; no longer having two funnels and with a newly shaped bow, she was even more attractive.

In 1939 she was refitted to become an Armed Merchant Cruiser with several guns. This took place in Simon's Town, South Africa. The captain at that time was HWM Hardy.

RMS Caernarvon mainly served in the South Atlantic against the Germans. She had a particular battle which was quite fierce, causing damage. However, she was able to proceed to Montevideo for some temporary repairs before returning to Simon's Town for permanent ones.

She was refitted in USA when radar was installed and then, in 1944, she was given another refit, this time as a troopship serving the route between America and South Africa. She still had about 1,283 berths when Mother, Lindsey and I sailed on board from Cape Town to England!

She was again modernized and returned to the Mail Service between South Africa and the UK until she was scrapped in 1962.

Leaving South Africa in the warmth of summer, November 1946, we sailed northwards into winter, with the days growing progressively colder. There was very little space to sit anywhere, and getting cold, we passengers often used the blankets from our bunks to try to keep warm when on deck. I remember rather enjoying the canteen meals, each of us having a little tray with indentations for the main course and vegetables and then a sweet; it all seemed so well organised!

There were some lovely nuns in our cabin, who were very sweet to us. Mother found she could really talk with them and, I think, told them quite a lot about the past years and all the uncertainties for the future. They promised to pray for us, and sometimes, in the months that followed, when trusting that our lives would become more settled, we would remind each other of these dear nuns' prayers. It was a very comforting thought and I am sure we had many wonderful answers, especially about our schooling and Mother travelling to China.

The arrival at Dover seemed chaotic – crowds of people milling about uncertainly, sorting luggage, and papers, forms, and money. It was a cold, dull, foggy day in November, and somehow not welcoming! Mother bought tickets for the Pullman Train, and we were thankful to get seats and to be on our way to London. Here we were met by Father's brother, Uncle Vince, and his wife, Aunt Teen, with a lovely warm welcome! Mother realised that there was a missing piece of luggage which Uncle Vince kindly helped her to find, and Aunt Teen took us to Watford to Granny's house.

We had been to this house before, but now it seemed so tiny! Granny had her sister, Aunt Tot, living with her. She must have been quite a bit her elder and was blind with lots of problems; she kept to her room, so we did not see much of her. I thought it was wonderful of Granny to squeeze us all in and that it was so good to be with her again. The garden seemed minute; it had the large mound of a Morrison shelter built into the grass where there had been a lawn, and the little apple trees were shrouded with mist.

It's alright now – God is in charge!

It must have been very sad for Granny not to see Father again, but she obviously was glad she could see us. I felt so sorry too that Father did not have the opportunity to return to England and that it would be a long time before his next leave; that was hard on the whole family.

Father's sister, Joyce, her husband, Jack, and our cousins John, Hilary and two-year-old Ralph invited us all to tea at their home nearby. Here we had the most marvellous meal! We were amazed at all the delicious cakes and biscuits. It was a truly memorable meal; after the shortages in quite a different way in South Africa, it made me feel that England was not as bad as we had heard! It was only later that I realised that this dear family must have saved their coupons to be so generous, and then I felt quite awed! John and Hilary were about the same ages as Lindsey and I and it was so interesting to hear about their very different schooling and way of life. I know this made me feel rather daunted; would we ever be able to reach their standard in French, Latin or Maths, I wondered! We had done none of these subjects before, and the only history we had studied was about South Africa and the explorations of Vasco de Gama, for instance, and the Great Trek and the Boer Wars. I could see that our education so far was woefully inadequate!

We went for a pleasant walk in Cassiobury Park with our cousins, which was really nice – until Lindsey and I tried to retrieve a ball from a patch of nettles and learnt the hard way how nettles sting! There was obviously much to learn about in England!

Shortly after this Mother, Lindsey and I stayed with Penny in Norfolk, much to our delight. It was wonderful to see Penny again even though she kept exclaiming how much we had grown and how our dear little round faces at the age of six had now become much longer and so different! We then all went on to stay for the Christmas holidays with Mother's brother, Jim, his wife, Sally, and our cousins Brendan, Richard and Isabel at St Ives, near Cambridge. This was such a happy time and much appreciated by us all. Brendan and Richard were each at Cambridge University, doing very well both academically and in sport, earning blues in rowing, their commemorative oars being displayed on the living room wall. Isabel was about our age, and we got on very happily together.

Soon after Christmas there was some severe flooding from the burst river banks over fields nearby, and we had such fun in a little boat going to explore the new landscape now under water. I was impressed when Mother, who had not ridden a bicycle for a great many years, courageously went for a ride – but how she regretted this after finding it was exhausting, and how stiff she felt later! Lindsey and I had ridden horses but never a bike, and again felt lacking in this apparently essential skill. Presently, with her new term beginning, Isabel would cycle to her school, about a couple of miles away, in every weather condition; I admired this!

On our return to Penny's home, Garden Cottage, Necton, there was an earnest search for a school for Lindsey and me, many letters being written with much prayer and discussion. Eventually a school in Windsor was found, a school which would be able to take us and was aware of our shortfall in education.

A new uniform for this school had to be obtained, with other requirements too. We needed overalls, and some material was found to make these. We each had similar ones made in a cotton material with a tiny check of red, white and blue, and I remember not liking them at all! I wished we could have different clothes and colours from each other. Mother had always dressed us alike, and I do not think anyone realised how much I longed to be treated more as an individual. However, I understood that in England there was still so much rationing; everything was new and strange and we probably could not afford very much anyway, as far as I could tell. I can't remember at this stage of our lives whether we had regular pocket money, but the list of necessities at this school included a particular amount of pocket money for the boarders.

We talked quite a lot about Mother joining Father in Tientsin, and Mother was also searching for a passage on a ship going out to China. It was difficult to think about the huge changes that were taking place in all our lives at this time. In fact, I do not believe that we actually discussed this very much; in those days there was so much happening that in some ways it probably seemed just another way of life!

I had said to Mother, very earnestly, when we were staying with Granny, that now we were nearly thirteen it would be alright for her to leave us in England and to join Father. I noticed the expression of sadness in her beautiful face as I voiced these thoughts. Much later, I clearly understood how hard it must have been to leave us at this new stage of our lives but also how much she longed to be with Father too. Plans were made for us to spend school holidays with Penny and her friend Enid Butters from the Volunteer Ambulance Drivers during the War. We were quite happy about that, knowing such security with these loving people, but I do not think it occurred to me at first how much we were going to miss Mother.

CHAPTER SEVENTEEN

Garden Cottage

Upton Preparatory School in Windsor was so different from schools in South Africa. We must have gone there first in February, 1947, and were installed in the Boarding House for the School at 25, Osborne Road, Windsor. This seemed quite pleasant, and here I particularly loved the sweet little younger girls and the view we had of Windsor Castle!

We soon settled into the school and began to enjoy most of the lessons, and the other girls, the staff and our new lives altogether. However, French, Latin and Maths were a great struggle as we were so far behind the other children. I remember Lindsey being rebellious in having to learn French from a children's book about rabbits! It just seemed a necessary way to start, somehow, and in the end I quite liked French – not that we did oral French at all, just the written part, in those days.

Then the time came for Mother to leave us and sail to China to join Father. She came to see us in Windsor before departing. She thought it would be lovely to take us for a carriage ride in Windsor Great Park going right up to the Memorial of King George the Third on the top of the hill, along the three mile driveway from the castle. And it was lovely, except we were all so aware of her having to leave us, that this was a 'goodbye' and that we were very sad indeed.

She sailed for China on her own by a Blue Funnel liner. It was very rough in the Mediterranean; she was severely sea-sick and then suffered an agonizing ear infection. Not that we knew all this until much later, but I am not surprised that Mother went through a very difficult time after all that she had experienced, with the many stresses and painful partings in her life. Also, she had heard that Father was near a breakdown and was very concerned, realising afresh how much he needed her. However, it was through a fellow passenger on board this ship that she heard about a Christian school – Clarendon, in North Wales – which took children whose parents were very often missionaries, children who had had poor education and possibly traumatic backgrounds.

Not much was discussed with us, but I think that the headmistresses at our school were quietly understanding about Mother leaving us in England to join Father in China. I especially liked Miss Winifred Drewe for her gentleness and for being a good teacher. Miss Joy was much more fun but perhaps not so sensitive. They each went to different churches in Windsor; Miss Drewe's church was Anglo-Catholic, and Miss Joy went to the main parish church. I enjoyed both these types of worship and realised that in the end it simply does not matter what kind of churchmanship there is, with all the differing ways of expression, as long as the people love the Lord Jesus.

Penny was officially our guardian while our parents were abroad, and we went back to Garden Cottage for the holidays. Garden Cottage was a delightful old cottage, originally built for the chief gardener who produced all the fruit and vegetables from its orchards and walled garden for the main house, Necton Hall. This gracious old Hall building was falling into disrepair but, at that time, it was possible for my aunt to rent the cottage. Enid, Penny's great friend, always would give up her larger bedroom for Lindsey and me, kindly moving into the tiny spare room. We saw how hard these two dear ladies worked in their market garden, really trying to make a living from it all with quite a lot of difficulty. I think they must have given up much time for us, and I am sorry that I did not fully appreciate this in those days. They had a three-wheeled vehicle which was just big enough for two people and the delivery of their garden produce. They always seemed cheerful, although they had so little of the usual comforts in life. As Necton Hall was no longer occupied, its generator was not functioning; so although the wiring was still in place in the cottage, there was no electricity, and neither was water laid on. Paraffin lamps and candles were our main sources of light, and water was pumped up by a pump with a handle in the kitchen from the well in the front garden. While this was quite a chore, at least it was something Lindsey and I could do! The radio was powered by a large and heavy battery and used very sparingly, mostly for the news bulletins, gardening programmes and Penny and Enid's favourite radio programme, 'ITMA'[37]. Heating was by an open fire – either in the dining-room or occasionally in the sitting room – and the old stove with its ovens in the kitchen.

The Kitchen, 1947
Remembered for years,
Even with tears,
An old fashioned kitchen
With a quarry tiled floor,
Without any windows –
Just a half-glazed door.
Looking round with inward eye,
I see again, so vividly,
The tiny kitchen sink
Plumbed into corner dark,
Or so I used to think,
With a tiny little draining board,
That always was too small!
Then, beside the larder door,
Installed upon the wall,
Was the ancient hand-pump –
That demanding overlord!
One hundred times
The pump was pulled,
Drawing water from the well,
One hundred times at least,
An urgent task
That must not cease!
Next, there stood a wooden table,
Covered with a sheet of lino,
Concealing every crack,
Strong and durable
Withstanding all attacks
Of implements and instruments
So necessary for cookery!

---

[37] "It's That Man Again!"

It's alright now – God is in charge!

Much discussion happened there,
With many questions asked,
Preparing us for life –
Such a useful mix,
From copying a fashion-book
The post-war style,
'New Look',
(Oh! That modernity!)
To careers and work,
And what to do in emergencies.
We talked so often
Of Christianity,
Of virtues and of vanities,
And how to be a wife.
We needed, too,
To learn some skills,
Like how to fill
The lamps with paraffin,
And carefully trim the wicks.
But it was the kitchen range
That commanded full attention!
It had a personality,
An awesome sort of dignity,
Demanding our respect.
When alive with red-hot coke,
And in an obliging mood,
It warmed and stewed and toasted,
And all the meals were good!
However, just occasionally,
It refused to do its best,
And then, sulking angrily,
Would bellow out its smoke
And, though we'd all object,
The meals were wrecked!
Such was 'home' in my teenage years,
A place remembered with grateful tears!

Once in nearly every holiday, Penny and Enid would take us to Norwich for shopping. It was quite a long journey by bus along the A47 and much enjoyed by us all, with the added treat of having a meal in a cafe somewhere. Having clothes rationing still, shopping was quite a challenge, and it was exciting when we came home triumphant with any successful purchases! Even handkerchieves needed coupons – and they were a must for the necessary school uniform. But sometimes, disappointingly, Enid would suffer a migraine just as we were about to go, and we would all stay at home with Penny lovingly taking care of her.

We went to a dentist in King's Lynn, and apart from the dentist we also enjoyed these visits. We were in a large shop once when there was quite a hush from everyone; I was standing by a particular counter when I suddenly realised Queen Mary was beside me. It was a memorable moment; she looked so regal and dignified with her upright posture and lovely hairdo. She and the Royal Family must have been staying at Sandringham at that time.

I liked the shops with their ways of sending money to the cashier at the till in the pipes overhead. There were no calculators then, of course, and there was something pleasant about the way shopkeepers related to their customers in what seemed an unhurried and courteous way.

There was not very much for us to do in Garden Cottage; I must have read almost every book on the shelves. But as the market-garden needed quite a lot of skilful work and as there wasn't the time to teach us these essential matters, we could not help much at all. Enid liked cooking, but I think she found that in a small kitchen with an erratic old Kit-Kat stove she preferred to prepare meals without our aid, so there wasn't much we could do there either. But we could do the shopping at the little village store, and that was some help. We also swept the living room carpets with the aid of tea-leaves which, so we learnt, assist in picking up dust! The baker still delivered the bread with his horse and wagon, and the friendly postman, Percy, with his wobbly false teeth, still came on his ancient bike, cheerfully handing us any letters – and especially the ones from our parents.

Necton was a small rural village, but we never felt part of it, neither did we make any friends there. Penny and Enid were far too hard-working to be able to join in with any activities or life in the village, and apart from the church, the post office and the shop, we did not visit it much. The village shop was run by two delightful ladies and was a very interesting place, with an assortment of strong smells. It seemed to sell everything necessary for everyone from the housewives and children to the farmers. It was impressively packed with a great variety of items: wellington boots hung from the ceiling; potatoes, kept in large baskets; sewing thread; skeins of wool; and large containers full of commodities – flour, tea, sugar, etc. Sugar would be carefully weighed out and poured into either blue or brown paper bags; these bags were prized by Penny and Enid for selling fruit or vegetables requested by any of the villagers who would come to Garden Cottage. Shopping was an entertaining experience, and I liked hearing the attractive Norfolk accent, although I have never succeeded in achieving this myself! Going to the butcher was not such fun. This was a solemn time with an atmosphere of seriousness concerning the purchases; because of the continuing rationing, difficult decisions would have to be made!

Penny and Enid told us how they would swap ration coupons for tea with people who did not want their cheese rations, so there had always been a little bartering, apparently! Ration Books were still playing an important role in everyone's lives. I was particularly horrified over the tiny amount of butter allowed because, of course, at The Hope there was no such shortage. Our meagre ration would be carefully cut into seven slices by Enid, one for each day of the week. This could be supplemented with margarine, but that offered no comparison to my mind and was not liked by me at all!

Penny and Enid were marvellous in every way, including teaching Lindsey and me to ride their ageing bicycles, endlessly patient and encouraging! We were glad when we mastered this skill and felt much more mobile and confident!

Penny and Enid had an adorable Bedlington Terrier, Tim, whom we all loved dearly. They had trained him not to walk on flower-beds, and if one of them wanted the other to have him they would just shout, "Call him!" and he would rush off to find her! This certainly was most helpful at times!

We would all go to the Necton Parish Church on Sundays, and I loved hurrying along the country lane, past the ponds where we had 'skated' in the freezing winter when I was aged five, through the farm gates and to the church, with the sound of the pealing bells, thinking this was really special! Penny and Enid both took Sunday School classes, and I believe they were a lovely influence in the village. The old church is beautiful and, amongst other things, has outstanding hammer-beam rafters. Gan-Gan had been buried in the churchyard, and we would lay flowers on her grave and keep it tidy.

One Easter holiday Lindsey and I went to Winchester to visit the Rix family – Eileen and her two sons – who had been with us in the Cameron Highlands. It was great to catch up with them, and we really appreciated this visit, although I have since regretted not sharing memories of our escapes from Malaya; I would have loved to have heard *their* story! Eileen's husband had died by this time, but they had met up safely with each other in India after the fleeing from Malaya. They took us to Winchester Cathedral – such a wonderful place with a very interesting history – and we saw a completely different part of England, which I found intriguing.

I liked Windsor very much too: the Castle with its ancient history; the stout ramparts and walls; the keep with the flags flying in the wind; and sometimes the Royal Standard, when the Royal Family were in residence. I loved Windsor Great Park and the town itself, the Thames at Eton and the pleasure of watching the boats, especially when it was 4th June, Eton's great day.

When there were special events at Windsor Castle we would go to the grounds behind the castle to watch the shows, and once saw the princesses, Elizabeth and Margaret, much to everyone's delight. We also went to a particular place where the Royal Family and their guests would change from travelling in their cars to ride in the carriages bound for the Royal Ascot Races – this was very special! And I loved the horses, especially the Windsor Greys.

We played netball in the Spring Term and started to play tennis in the Summer Term. I also loved being a Girl Guide with all the various activities. In fact, there was much going for us all at Upton Prep School, and we were mostly happy there. The Autumn Term with the preparations for Christmas delighted me; I so enjoyed the carols, and hearing some new ones was lovely too.

One Christmas we were all invited to join the Butters, Enid's family at Leiston, in Suffolk. Not having a big enough car for us all, it was decided that we would use the bikes and travel two by two, taking it in turns whether to cycle on Penny 's and Enid's bikes or go in the little vehicle. Enid and Lindsey cycled for the first miles, and then Penny and I exchanged places with them. This worked very well, and we all felt it was quite an achievement! It was a lovely Christmas and much enjoyed by everyone. Mr Butters was a charming man, a retired vicar, who could read and translate Greek into English simultaneously; Lindsey and I were very impressed!

Then – what joy! – we received the invitation to join the confirmation classes with several other members of our form at school. We were prepared by the young curate of All Saints Church, Frances Road, and he was very helpful. It was a rather 'high church', and before the Confirmation Service we had an opportunity to go to Confession. I dreaded this, having such a long list of sins to cope with! When the time came, the curate asked us in turn to come to the Lady Chapel where he was seated on the other side of the communion rail. He showed us a hassock where we could kneel at right angles to him, facing a crucifix on the wall. We reminded ourselves that these sins were committed by ourselves and that it was by our own fault only. I knelt with my lengthy list and very meaningfully, sadly confessed each thing to our Lord Jesus. I waited apprehensively to see what my penance would be and was grateful to find that I was just requested to go back to my seat in the church and to say the Lord's Prayer. What a relief! The other girls duly took their turn and then we all filed out of the church, quite happily, standing in a little group together.

Then, suddenly, I was infused with a tremendous joy. I felt as light as a feather – as though my feet were not even touching the ground – and had the amazing understanding that I was totally forgiven by our Lord Jesus! This was a wonderful experience for which I will always be grateful. I looked round; no one else was showing anything so I felt I must try to seem just as normal too!

Our confirmation was taken by the Dean of Windsor, The Rt Rev Eric Hamilton, and was lovely. We all wore white dresses – not so easy to find in the days of clothes rationing! My dear godmothers, Penny and Marian Knight, were both at the service, and that was very special to me. I hoped so much that something really marvellous would happen at the actual laying-on-of-hands but, frankly, was rather disappointed! However, after this we were able to have the real privilege of receiving communion, and I really loved that! I had thought, reading the Bible, that there would be evidence of the Holy Spirit, with the gifts as well as the fruit, but was told rather firmly that "all that happened in those Bible story days was a sort of 'scaffolding' to help the early Church; nowadays we have hospitals and doctors to take care of the sick." I pondered on this for many years and could not quite believe it; in the Bible Jesus says he is the same yesterday, today and forever, and somehow I knew this is still the truth and that surely he still answers prayer and heals the sick!

Quite soon after this, I had another amazing dream, and for the first time I understood our Lord Jesus' second coming! I felt myself going upwards, along with many, many people, into glorious light and colour, and wonderful music, angels and joy! I knew I was going *home*, in an amazing way, and experienced something of the real presence of Jesus! It was all so vivid and beautiful – and true! There was no one with whom I felt I could share this astonishing dream; how I missed my Mother! Then I had an opportunity to tell Miss Drewe at school; she was so sweet and understanding, and encouraging as well, and that was a blessing!

Sometimes my godmother, Marian Knight, would take Lindsey and me out for the day – always a treat! She and her husband, Jeff, lived in Harrow, and occasionally we would also stay with them. Uncle Jeff was very musical, and they would have delightful musical gatherings at their home with their friends, which we would also enjoy. Marian liked baking and would produce the most delicious cakes for these occasions! They had an Airedale dog called Michael (but always known as 'Micksie'). He was allowed to lick any plates or dishes after meals, but Marian said, as she poured hot water over all the washing-up later, that then everything would be really clean! I sometimes had my doubts! We loved Aunt Anne, Marian's mother, who lived with them and who was especially sweet and loving to us. She would give us one shilling and six pence to go to the cinema sometimes – another much appreciated treat!

Bertha Haggard, Lindsey's godmother, also took us out, and once I remember we were very impressed with her new car – she was so thrilled with it! It was difficult for Penny and Enid to visit us from Norfolk, which was very understandable, but we especially appreciated their visits whenever this was possible.

It was always good to get back to school life and our friends after the holidays, and then it was lovely to return to Norfolk for the summer holidays. One summer we joined Penny, Enid and Enid's sisters, Hilda and Gwen, and set off by ferry to St Malo for a holiday at Erquy in Brittany! This was such a pleasure, and I loved this little coastal town and the beauty of the scenery. We stayed in a pleasant little French boarding house, and for the first time I heard French being spoken fluently. I enjoyed the warm croissants, the soups and new French dishes very much. We would all go for walks over the headlands, loving exploring some of the pretty coastline enthusiastically – that is, until we met a mad dog! Hilda, who had a walking stick, fended him off firmly as he barked in a most bloodthirsty way. The rest of us all sheltered behind her, allowing her to be our pivot, feeling a bit safer from this vantage position, swinging in a long line of terrified spectators wherever she moved! It may not have been such a long time, but eventually a man appeared, attracted by the ferocious barking and, quite likely also, by the anxious squeals of the line of ladies, and kindly rescued us!

Mother and Penny were praying about the next school that would be right for us after Upton Preparatory School and started looking at all the information they could find. There was much correspondence between them. Penny took us to see a school in East Sussex; I remember enjoying the train journey, but none of us liked the atmosphere in the school, and I was glad we did not go there. They then heard from Mother about Clarendon School, which at that time was in Malvern. On writing to Miss Swain, the Headmistress, they were informed that the school was moving to North Wales and that there would be places for us there. It was decided that that would be the best school; everything about it seemed so right – it was Christian and also would help us to continue catching up with much that we had missed in our education!

Chapter Eighteen

Clarendon

larendon School was set amongst the hills south of Abergele in North Wales, a very beautiful situation with marvellous views. The old Kinmel Hall was an attractive building in lovely grounds and made a great venue for the new school! Because the building was not quite ready for us all, the first term started late, so Lindsey and I were still at Garden Cottage in May, experiencing the wonder of this very special season. I was enchanted with the beauty of the garden, the huge variety of scented flowers and blossoms. I particularly enjoyed the chestnut trees with their spectacular 'candles' and, most of all, the nightingales singing in the woods nearby. Although I looked forward to starting at Clarendon School, there was some reluctance in leaving such loveliness behind!

Penny was going to accompany us to North Wales. First we would stay with Kit Pennell, Lindsey's godmother in Liverpool. It was good to meet Aunt Kit; she had been one of Mother's very special friends before her marriage to Father and had married Captain Pennell who was the captain of the ship that Scott of the Antarctic had travelled on, a story I wanted to know much more about.

Almost immediately on our arrival at Aunt Kit's house, we were asked to take Aunt Kit's little Fox Terrier for a walk; so using his lead we set off on unknown roads with the little 'stranger', who turned out to be quite a handful! He suddenly had alarming hysterics, but Lindsey had the presence of mind to cover his head with a jersey, calming him down. I don't think either of us enjoyed our walk and were glad to find the way back to his home!

It's alright now – God is in charge!

On the following day it was exciting to see something of Liverpool and the Liverbirds as we caught the ferry across the Mersey on our way to the train for Abergele. As our taxi drove from the station up to our new school, Penny told us how she and Enid as Voluntary Ambulance Drivers during the War, used to come to Kinmel Hall sometimes, when it had then become a hospital. On their return they would switch off their ambulance engines to coast down the mile long drive, so saving petrol – the ambulances only managing to do ten miles to the gallon!

We had our first glimpse of the magnificent building, modelled (as I learnt later) on the Palace of Versailles and built between 1871 and 1876. The taxi drove through the imposing wrought iron gates, rattled noisily over the sheep grid, and rolled up to the impressive front doors of our new school, tyres scrunching on the gravel in the large forecourt.

We were warmly greeted at once by members of the staff. As we were shown round this enormous building, we felt everything was going to be alright in the friendly atmosphere and began to relax. Penny was able to leave us also feeling confident, and I know we all realised that God had answered prayers again!

Everyone was 'new' together in this wonderful building. Somehow that was such a help, and it was fun to get lost and then find the right way with the other girls! There was much to explore! I think that our form room and dormitories were probably in what may have been the servants' quarters; however, they seemed pleasant, and our classroom was large, light and airy.

I was very impressed with what would have been the main reception rooms. They had magnificent proportions with arresting fireplaces, marble pillars, panelling, wood block floors and ornate plaster work. There was such a lot to see and admire! The huge main staircase attracted me, though this was only for the use of staff and senior girls. The steps were wide and fairly shallow; I could imagine the ladies of a past era dressed in beautiful gowns gracefully descending them! There was a little mezzanine sitting area at the top of the first flight of stairs, overlooking the lovely Venetian Rose Garden, and then there was a door which led into the old chapel, now the school library which was another very lovely place.

The windows seemed so tall, and from them the surrounding landscapes were endlessly enjoyed, from the distant hills and the sea to woodlands on the rising slopes of nearby hills and, closer still, the sheep with their lambs in the parkland round about. The grounds immediately surrounding the house were beautiful. There were about eighteen acres of walled gardens, with many fine specimen of trees and wonderful places which we gradually discovered. There was a sunken drive with a bridge built over it, and we found that 'The Venetian Garden' was really outstanding, with features such as circular fountains and small ornate trees carefully kept in attractive shapes. Here there would be gatherings for special occasions and photos taken. Later, in the Sixth Form, some classes would even be held there; I particularly remember enjoying English Literature sitting with our group on some sun-warmed stone steps!

The Headmistress' large drawing room, overlooking the Venetian Garden, was most attractive, and here Miss Swain always had an adorable stuffed lion family lying on the carpet in a charming friendly way! We used to gather there to have special times listening to her reading inspiring stories to us while we sewed and embroidered articles, some of which would be sold at the School's Open Day in the summer in aid of the Bethnal Green Mission.

So I loved Clarendon School, sometimes feeling in my delight that I just wanted to hug the building where I was beginning, perhaps for the first time, to have a sense of security in a school and also in England! I loved the Christian ethos and appreciated the feeling that everything was prayed over and under the authority of God. Of course there were many new rules, but they seemed fair and reasonable on the whole!

The day started with a ten minute 'Quiet Time' for prayer and Bible reading, before the exercises in our House groups on the forecourt. The girls were each a member of one of the six Houses, named after famous Christian women. Mine was Slessor – Mary Slessor, who bravely worked in Nigeria in the last century. Our House Leaders would organise the various exercises with varying degrees of enthusiasm, and I am sure we all tried to follow her obediently. We would then proceed to breakfast where two of the staff, standing at the entrance of the dining room, would greet each girl personally as she came in. Breakfast was really welcome by then!

We would be given a seat in the dining room at the beginning of term, and we stayed in the order planned for us with the same neighbours, but moving one place round each table every day so that we would also move gradually around the dining room, with a different member of staff at the head of each table. It seemed a good idea and worked well, although I rather dreaded the French teachers' table because, of course, we would have to attempt to speak French! We were not supposed to ask for anything, such as butter, to be passed to us but were encouraged to look after neighbours. This led to some queries, "Would you like some butter?" even though it was apparent that the other already had this but hopefully stimulating the realisation that that was what you needed!

Beds were to be completely stripped every day, the mattresses turned and then made again exactly according to the rules, in order that the bedrooms looked amazingly neat, with the counterpanes folded correctly. We were taught how to keep the bedrooms, bathrooms and corridors clean, each girl being allotted a task, and there were high standards to reach in the half hour we were given. There was a system of stars and stripes given according to behaviour in any situation, and these went towards our Houses, so careful cleaning really mattered. Excellent results could earn stars, but it was awful if you received a stripe! I remember receiving this once due to "a hair in hair brush"!

Morning assembly with prayers and a hymn was held in the large Hall, which in the past would probably have been a wonderful ballroom. There was a gallery on the rear wall, I imagine for musicians, and which the girls would sometimes use as an overflow for seating if the Hall was very full on special occasions. We were very blessed with excellent musicians, either members of staff or senior girls, and enjoyed a lovely selection of hymns from 'Golden Bells' and CSSM Choruses. This time was a helpful preparation for the day's activities and lessons. Lindsey and I found we were still behind in many areas of the classes, especially Maths and French – Latin was firmly dropped – but I think we both found the teaching encouraging and, mostly, quite enjoyable! Besides the form rooms, some classes were also held in the attractive stable block, mainly art and geography at first, but other subjects also found their way to these interesting old buildings. These stables were built when the second Kinmel Hall was designed in the Palladian style matching the Hall, circa 1842-1843, and were not damaged in the fire which ruined the main house shortly after it had been built.

Life at this school was well organised and seemed very full; there were more and more activities planned, various societies and clubs were formed, and I believe most people were very happy. We looked forward to weekends and more free time. Of course there was shoe-polishing and various chores to be done and always the important letter writing to parents; but then there were delightful walks or cycle rides, and so many places to see and visit. And we had the pleasure of sweets on Saturdays and Sundays! We were allowed to have six sweets on a Saturday and eight on a Sunday after lunch, carefully chosen from our own tuck boxes! The rules relaxed a bit as one became more senior, but there was still rationing; this was also evident in that we were not given sugar for our tea and our meals were fairly simple, although well thought out and excellent.

Every Sunday there were inspiring services held in the Assembly Room with very good talks and always the singing of lovely hymns. Clarendon was of the 'low-church' spectrum, quite different from the school in Windsor but also based on truth and the Word of God. Miss Swain was from the Brethren Church, as were several of the staff and girls; others would go to the Baptist Church in a nearby town, and many of us went to the little church in the neighbouring village, St George, at one of the Kinmel Park gates. There was an opportunity there to receive communion after the morning service, and Lindsey and I would stay behind for this.

However, the fact that we had been confirmed already did not seem to meet with much approval; weren't we too young for that? I thought this was rather bewildering! Then we found we could go to the 8am Holy Communion Service which, I think, was held once a month. I loved the walk through the park with the freshness of an early summer morning, the beauty of the scenery and the enchanting little lambs bleating for their mothers until they found them again with joyful reunions! And I so loved the peace and meaning of that wonderful little service.

We were all invited by one of my friends to her Baptism Ceremony. I found it most interesting and felt that this was surely how it was in the Bible and longed to have the experience of total immersion too! Several decades later I did have the opportunity to be baptised like this and was deeply blessed and very grateful!

There were plenty of opportunities for games in their due seasons, with hockey and cricket in the ample space in the parkland and several good courts for tennis. I enjoyed hockey but was never confident about tennis! We were encouraged to join the various teams; games were usually played in the afternoons before tea and homework.

Our form will always remember our Midnight Feast held in the grounds in the old Cricket Pavilion! I think the staff must have kindly turned a blind eye to what was going on so secretly, and the event was a great success and such fun!

The senior girls took quite a bit of responsibility as prefects, and all this aided the smooth functioning of day-to-day life. There was one surprising weekend in each year when the staff were 'off duty' and the prefects took their places, often with hilarious results, which everyone enjoyed very much and also proved to be quite a helpful incentive in many ways.

Every year there would be special days when parents could come and see the school, their children's work, and hear the excellent concerts which had been very carefully rehearsed, and beautifully delivered in the Assembly Hall. They could also watch the displays of complicated marches performed on the great expanse of the forecourt. One of the gifted pupils would play the piano for some of the events, and I think we all took great pride in these lovely occasions. Sometimes we would have a sale for the Christian outreach work in Bethnal Green and be very pleased with the results made from the stalls of our embroidery or craftsmanship, when I am sure parents would have been very generous!

Naturally our own parents were not able to come to these special events, but the time came at last for Father to take his Home Leave, and to our immense joy both our precious parents returned to England! They had just had a further trauma in China, having to leave nearly all their newly acquired possessions because of the turmoil there under Chiang Kai-Shek and his army. Having lost almost everything in Singapore as well, my parents enjoyed their 'things' but realised that these are not so very important and often very transitory!

We met in London again at the start of the summer holidays, and Father told us of plans to take a house on the Norfolk Broads where we could explore and have boats to sail! This was a wonderful idea to us! We had had a couple of marvellous weeks with Christian groups sailing on the Broads on two Easter holidays previously and were thrilled with this plan! Father also said he was giving us each a bicycle, another delight!

These holidays were very special and we thoroughly enjoyed 'The Thatched Cottage' right on the river at Horning. Father hired a half-decker yacht, the 'Olive May', and we had such fun learning how to sail. We particularly enjoyed meeting another family with Susan Wilson and her brothers of similar ages to us, and the friendly races against each other's yachts. Bishop Leonard Wilson was acting as locum for the Vicar of Horning that summer, staying in the vicarage with his family; he was then the Bishop of Birmingham, who had previously been the Bishop of Singapore and had suffered terribly under the Japanese as a P.O.W. but had wonderfully forgiven his torturers. He and Father had several long talks, and I believe that this was a real help to Father in beginning also to be forgiving.[38]

Father also hired a cabin cruiser for a week; we discovered further beautiful areas of the Broads and had an incident in which we faced the well-known problem of negotiating the narrow arch of Potter Heigham Bridge – and got it wrong! But somehow being at such close quarters with Father seemed to bring difficulties, and we realised he could be quite unreasonable with marked mood changes. There were also times when Father had horrific nightmares and when he apparently needed to be on his own and seemed very upset. This was quite distressing for us to see. It was not a new situation, but it was so helpful that Mother always remained calm and understanding.

We had several relations to stay, one by one as there wasn't that much space in the little cottage. Cousins John, Brendan and Mera came. Penny and Enid visited us too, which was a huge pleasure.

---

[38] Very much later the Bishop's brother, Leslie Wilson, became the Vicar of Malacca and officiated at Hugh's and my wedding!

Father, happy and relaxed, sailing on the Norfolk Broads on leave in 1948

Lindsey's godmother, Bertha Haggart, also came. She was a well-known pianist and sweetly explained that she did not want to hold the oars of our little boat when we took her for an excursion because she had to look after her hands carefully. We were so impressed and realised how important her piano playing was to her. In every way this was a special summer, and then it was so good that our parents did not return to the Far East until after the Christmas holidays.

One of the emphases in the services at school, we found, was making sure that we had asked the Lord Jesus into our hearts and lives. I had not heard about becoming a Christian in this way and thought about it a lot, but I decided that in many ways I really knew Jesus through my remarkable dreams and experiences of answered prayer and felt confident that I was already a Christian. Sometimes we were asked when it was that we had asked the Lord into our hearts, and I found this query quite difficult – when was it exactly? I could not be sure, and this made me rather reticent! But I knew that I knew Jesus in a very real way!

The Christmas term would end with a marvellous celebration contributed by the staff from Europe, with beautiful decorations and a very special meal – memorable in every way! And every term would be completed with a certain ritual: a hurried early breakfast, prayers for the wellbeing of us all, Psalm 21, and then, just before catching our trains, singing the meaningful chorus:

Kept by the Power of God,
Kept by the Power of God,
Day by day,
Come what may,
Kept by the Power of God

Just after we had taken 'School Certificate', Lindsey and I flew out to Malaya for the summer holidays, where we were to join our parents. This was such an adventure to us and a never-to-be-forgotten experience! Marian and Jeff kindly took us to Northholt to catch our plane. We were flying with BOAC on one of the very first flights of children to join their families in the Far East, and were really thrilled! All the children met in a large, temporary building that had been used for the air force during World War II, and we found the staff so helpful, living up to their slogan "BOAC takes good care of you!" It was exciting to board the Argonaut aircraft and fly into the night. As we flew through the valleys of the Alps – not above them! – there was a thunder storm with dramatic flashes of lightning illuminating the mountain sides, very beautiful and a little bit scary! We landed in Cairo where we found that the Egyptian staff were a little too interested in the young girls, and we were relieved when, after refuelling, we embarked again to fly to Karachi. It was amazing to pass over the Saudi Arabian desert and to be able to make out Israel in the far distance, on a startlingly clear day. The plane had comfortable seats and also an area with a table, where we could sit and chat to other teenagers, above the sounds of the very noisy engines! After setting off again from Karachi we flew southwards along the west coast of India, and the pilot invited anyone who would be interested to come, in turns, to the cockpit. I was thrilled with this visit and was astonished to be allowed to handle the controls and to steer the plane – under very eagle-eyed supervision! This was another memorable experience!

We spent a night in Colombo, where my parents had arranged that Hong Kong and Shanghai Bank friends of theirs would look after us! They were kind and took us to watch a tennis match, which I hate to say, I don't think either Lindsey or I appreciated – sitting in the hot sunshine of the tropics, tired after the long flight, watching unknown players competing in a match, did not appeal very much just then! Thankfully, looking back I am fairly sure that we would have been too shy to express our feelings!

We landed in Singapore the following day and were gladder than I can say to be with our dear parents again after such a long time! Mother took us shopping for much needed summer wear, and Father bought us each a lovely crocodile skin handbag! We drove up to Muar the next day in their Austin A40 car, crossing over the causeway to Johore Bahru, intrigued by the different scenery, the crops of pineapple, the palm trees, the banana groves, the enchanting Malay kampongs (villages) with pretty houses on stilts and thatched roofs. We crossed the river at Batu Pahat on a ferry manned by Indian men spitting out red betel-nut juice and shouting important but unintelligible instructions to one another. Finally, we arrived happily at our destination, weary and hot and delighted with the thought of the long summer holidays ahead.

I kept thinking how lovely it was to be back in this beautiful country so soon after the war and, although this was at the beginning of The Emergency, apparently there still was no real threat from the Communist terrorists; the country seemed to be quietly getting organised again and appeared to be so peaceful. I wondered what the conditions had been like for all these dear Malayan people in WWII. I was just beginning to grasp a little of what it had been like for Father – Father never talked about his experiences to us.

We would often drive to Malacca (about twenty miles away) where there was a delightful seawater swimming pool, attractively situated beside the beach, with a huge thatched roof over a very pleasant seating area, where delicious meals were served. Soon I had the thrill of learning to drive with the nicest of Malay syces, Abdullah, whose work was to drive my parents when necessary and to keep the car in good condition. He made two large signs for learner drivers, which looked impressive until one suddenly realised that the 'L' was reversed! It did not seem too important to point this out to him at the time, so Lindsey and I would gaily take it in turn to have our lessons! I loved this, confidently driving along wide avenues almost empty of traffic and becoming used to handling the car. It was great!

Mother had made their home so attractive and it was such a joy to be with her. In the background, always, Father would play records of wonderful classical music; how I loved that! The dear syce gave Lindsey and me a little white kitten, who was sweet... until she started climbing up everything she could find, seemed deaf, and was strangely mad and wild! We found, to our embarrassment, that we could not handle her and sadly gave her back. I understood that Mother was very relieved!

Instead of baths we had a huge jar of water, and in the hot climate it was wonderfully refreshing to pour cold water over ourselves with the aid of a special cup; this 'mandy' was always much appreciated!

Father took some local leave, and we stayed in a beautiful house near the Malacca Swimming Club at Tanjong Kling. It was lovely here, and we were all so happy together. Malacca itself is an interesting old town with a history of Portuguese trading, battles and conquests. There is an attractive old church[39] in the centre and several old buildings nearby of Dutch origin, some of which had been built about two hundred years earlier. These buildings are coloured a vibrant red, the influence of betel-nut juice! We liked all the delicious fruit very much, especially the mango-steens, pumaloes, and ripe bananas straight off the trees, but the smell of durian was so off-putting that I was never tempted to try any!

This was a very special holiday, and we so enjoyed everything, feeling grateful to have been able to come. On our flight back to England, we had the delight of landing near Rome and being taken by coach on a sightseeing tour, where we had fascinating glimpses of well-known places. It was another marvellous experience, but we always loved seeing our school friends again, so on our return there was much to tell them all and it was good to hear their news too. We were now in the Lower Sixth Form and enjoyed our new Form Room very much; it had been one of the reception rooms in the previous days and such a gracious room, overlooking the front of Kinmel Hall and the forecourt.

By this time, however, I was suffering from some condition which the doctors had not been able to help me with. I would get quite severe headaches and feel very ill at times. I had had my eyes tested and several other examinations, but the cause had not been found. I began to wonder if some of the staff thought I was 'malingering' and felt so unhappy about this! I had had a bad bout of flu' some time earlier and wondered if that had contributed to this malaise at all – but the unpleasant symptoms persisted. In the end it was decided that I should leave school after the end of that year because I was missing so many classes and just was not well. I was most upset about this, although I could see it was for the best.

It was at this time that I turned more and more to our Lord Jesus and, as always, this was such a help. I looked up everywhere in the Bible about God loving us, and that was a deep comfort to me; there is a wonderful amount of amazing verses of reassurance, which was just what I needed!

At one particularly inspiring service, just a little before I left school, we sang the hymn, "When I survey the wondrous cross on

---

[39] Hugh and I were married at this church

176

which the Prince of Glory died", concluding with the words, "Love so amazing, so divine, demands my life, my soul, my all." It was suggested that instead of singing "demands" in that line, we should sing "shall have".

Afterwards I was able to be quietly in my bedroom on my own. I knelt by the open window overlooking the beautiful Venetian Garden and prayed with all my heart those words again. I felt it might seem a little formal because I knew Jesus was my Saviour, in every sense of that wonderful word. But very solemnly I gave my whole life into His hands, trusting Him over my future, any work or training He wanted me to do, my husband (if I should marry), my children (if I should have any) – in fact, every possible part of me and my life ahead. As I knelt I knew this prayer was heard and realised an amazing depth of peace and assurance. [40]

The year had passed quite quickly, and I was really sorry to say goodbye to my dear friends and this lovely school. But there was one last memorable experience first: every year Clarendon School would host the CIM Conference (the China Inland Mission) and the Sixth Forms were invited to stay at the start of the summer holidays for these special days, to look after the guests! We would wait at table and do anything else required of us, with the real privilege of meeting some of these inspiring missionaries from China. I was deeply impressed by an outstanding person who was filled with the love of God and thrilled that he seemed to want to get to know us, taking a great interest in individuals and sharing something of his own work and faith.

Lindsey and I were to fly out to Malaya again for the summer holidays, and I felt sure I would still be able to keep in touch with special friends. What I did not know then was, of course, that it would be several years before I returned to England and how

---

[40] Some decades later Hugh and I stayed at Kinmel hall, after it had been converted to a Conference Centre, for a wonderful Christian gathering. It was just amazing for me to return to this beautiful place, to walk round the grounds, enjoy the Venetian Garden, and visit all my special places! I was able to go into the bedroom where I had prayed so deeply about my future; kneeling again at the same window, I poured out my thanks for the way our Lord Jesus had led me, for my happy marriage and precious children, and telling Him how grateful I was for all His faithfulness over the years!

It's alright now – God is in charge!

different my life was to become! However it would be wonderful to be with my parents for a longer time and especially to get to know Father better at last.[41]

---

[41] About forty years after leaving school we had a Form Reunion in London where I met many of my dear Clarendon friends again. This was such fun; we decided that we would not wear name badges or anything like that although, of course, our appearances had changed over all those years! But we did quickly know each other again, sometimes by the profile or a laugh, the voice or a gesture; it was just marvellous! Naturally I had kept up with several close friends, but this was a very special occasion! Later on we all had an invitation to meet again at a school in North Wales fairly near Kinmel Hall where we were able to have the use of a new boarding house for girls. Those of us who accepted this invitation met happily again and found this was a momentous time of deep fellowship – truly remarkable. As a result, one of these lovely friends offered us hospitality in her own home in North Wales, but naturally her accommodation is rather limited so those of us who had been enthusiastic over the first invitation were invited to join her again. We find such wonderful fellowship always, and now we try to meet every couple of years. This is always such a tremendous joy!

CHAPTER NINETEEN

Life Changes

*I*t was 1951, and Father was to work in the Cameron Highlands in the State of Pahang; this would be his last post before retirement. The Hong Kong and Shanghai Bank had considerately thought about Mother, who always found that the tropical heat of Malaya affected her health and that the Cameron Highlands was a wonderfully suitable place for her. I believe the Hong Kong and Shanghai Bank were also considerate towards their employees who had suffered as P.O.W.s in the Far East, so again the Cameron Highlands seemed ideal at this point in both my parents' lives. It certainly was marvellous for Lindsey and me to come to such a beautiful situation for the 1951 summer holidays!

We enjoyed this time tremendously and loved being with our parents again, learning to play golf with Father, finding some beautiful walks and enjoying bird-watching with Mother; it was all so interesting! However, conditions in Malaya had altered tremendously since our last visit with what was known as the 'Malayan Emergency', a period of unrest following the creation of the Federation of Malaya (precursor of Malaysia) in 1948. As it impacted our lives considerably I will explain a bit about it.

The Malayan Emergency

The Malayan Emergency (1948-1960) was a form of guerrilla warfare and caused much disruption to Malaya resulting in hardship and many deaths. The word 'emergency' was used rather than 'war' for insurance purposes because insurers would not have honoured policy holders if it had been described as a 'war'. It began after WWII when the Federation of Malaya came into being. This was formed when several previous British territories joined together, including Sarawak and Sabah, and the establishment of a colonial government was worked out. These negotiations decided on special rights for Malays and also considered the positions of the Sultans, but these plans caused much anger to the Malayan National Liberation Army (known as MNLA), the armed part of the Malayan Communist Party (MCP) who wanted an independent communist Malaya. So they organised brutal attacks on police stations, tin mines, and rubber estates; they derailed trains and burned workers houses, murdering and causing havoc. In other words, this was guerrilla warfare, and in June 1948, the government declared a state of emergency.

The British and Commonwealth forces were deployed to deal with this insurgency; this is when many people served in the National Service and, amongst other challenges, learned about jungle warfare. The strategies used against the 'bandits', as the guerrillas became known, were unpopular. This was especially so of the organising of the 'New Villages'; the Chinese people, often in serious poverty, who lived in the 'ulu'[42] were forced to move to these unfamiliar places. However, the scheme began to work well; these people were no longer able to aid the bandits with food and other essentials, often against their will, and were better protected, recognising as time went by that in many ways they were better off with schools, health clinics and other assets.

The local High Commissioner, Sir Henry Gurney, was assassinated in February 1952, a shocking incident, after which Sir Gerald Templar was appointed to take over both the civil government and the military campaign. This was a great success; under his excellent leadership the new British High Commissioner began to cope with the political and economic unrest. He was always one of my heroes! In the early 1950's new ideas were put into action regarding local elections, having village councils and, importantly, many Chinese were given citizenship. These plans helped to lessen the support for the rebels and their communistic cause. Gradually the guerrilla initial successes faded away and many bandits began to

---

[42] 'jungle' in the Malay language

surrender; however, the emergency was only declared to be fully over in 1960, when it was officially announced that the communist uprising was defeated.

I remember, with a shudder, when one day Father, Lindsey and I decided to go for a walk behind our charming house, 'Mar Lodge', to see what the jungle was like on the hillside there. We were crashing our way through the undergrowth in between the densely packed trees, when we heard a loud angry shout, "Who goes there?" An indignant army officer, in charge of his platoon, was yelling furiously at us! He was incensed that we had been foolish enough to even think of entering such a potentially dangerous area! He warned that they might have shot us thinking we were terrorists! We all quickly learnt the lesson that the Emergency affected us too, and having previously been unaware that the innocent hillside behind the house could have held such threats, we never entered the jungle again!

We were quite limited as to where we could go in the Cameron Highlands in those days; the lovely tea plantations beyond, and further up the hills from the famous golf course, were out of bounds, as were many other areas, due to the Emergency. The flowers and wildlife were wonderful and overflowing with beauty, with so many varieties of birds, flowers and butterflies; it was all a sheer delight to see, and we would have loved to explore much more.

All too soon Lindsey returned to Clarendon School for her final year. For almost the first time in our lives, we were separated; this seemed strange to begin with, but I soon appreciated my independence, my new life and the new friends I made. I also found I enjoyed time to be alone and started to read the Bible more carefully. I was particularly interested in the stories of Jesus healing the sick and began to mark these passages with a green crayon, wondering why we didn't hear of such miracles these days.

There was no church in the Cameron Highlands at that time, but some services were held occasionally when Mother would often be asked to read from the Bible. I would be impressed always by her reverence for the Word and the meaningful way in which she read.

Another delight I always remember with pleasure was the lovely classical music Father constantly played on his gramophone.

Mother and I had many long talks about a great many things, and it was marvellous to catch up with so many aspects of life. I loved living with both my parents and still hoped very much to get to know Father better. He did not speak about his childhood much at all except to tell that he was encouraged to spend long hours on music practice! This must have made a big impression on him, and from other people's comments I believe he was an excellent piano player. His father died when Father was about thirteen years old; this made a huge difference to his family and left his mother quite impoverished. Father had an older brother, Vincent, and two younger sisters, Margaret (known as Peggy) and Joyce, and Father had to start working at an early age straight after leaving school. He found a position in a bank, beginning at the bottom rung; however, his small income was essential to his mother, and he was pleased to be able to help. Eventually he transferred to the Hong Kong and Shanghai Bank in London and it was there, much later, that he met Mother.

Because Father did not talk about his war experiences, I realise that I did not know enough about the situation to ask him the right questions to help him open up a bit more. It was only much later on that I began to learn more about the War while doing a lot of reading and research, and in particular, once in Norfolk, when I went with Father to Norwich to see Ronald Searle's drawings at an Exhibition with some models of P.O.W. camps in Thailand. He was very subdued and obviously did not feel able to discuss these amazing illustrations, finding the memories too painful. Much of this exhibition was an eye-opener to me, and I was deeply impressed, realising a little bit more of the dreadful deprivations suffered by the P.O.W.s.

In 1952, when now in the Cameron Highlands, we met 'Miss Griff', as she was always known. This wonderful lady, Anne Laugharne Phillips Griffeth-Jones, to give her full name, was head of the little Tanglin School. She was born in 1890, and in 1923 visited Singapore to see her brother. She loved it there so much that she wanted to stay. With no qualifications she started a tiny school with just a few pupils; this did so well that in 1934 she was persuaded to open a school in the Cameron Highlands. Again this flourished and soon there was a staff of twenty-two qualified teachers from England, and a hundred and fifty pupils. In those days children of British expatriates needed to be sent to England for their education, so it made such a difference that these children could stay at this school until aged about thirteen years. When Singapore fell to the Japanese in 1942, Miss Griff was interned with the women and children at the notorious Changi Prison. Because of her organisational skills and leadership she soon ran a school for the children in the prison. She said that she could – and did – forgive the Japanese for their cruel treatment of their prisoners but, of course, could not forget it. However there was one thing she found very hard: the Japanese withheld medication and she was very distressed after the War to find that there had been plenty of insulin which could have been given to the people suffering from diabetes, and who died in consequence.

Much later, I have discovered, she was awarded the OBE in 1958 for Services to Education, and then, in 1962, was given the PJK (Pingat Jasa Kebaktian) by the Sultan of Pahang for Meritorous Service.

She was obviously an outstanding lady! I have found that she died in Ipoh hospital in 1974 and that her grave is at Tapah at the base of the foothills of the Highlands she loved so much.

At the start of the new term I began to work as a 'classroom assistant' at Tanglin School. I enjoyed this very much, loving the little children and being delighted to help with their new skills of reading and writing. The Matron, Hester Todd, became a good friend and later would come to our Scottish dancing evenings whenever possible. She often spoke of her family in Edinburgh, of her nine siblings and particularly of her sister Allison who was married to a Richard Cassidy. Some of my jobs were sorting the laundry, folding the tiny clothes when helping her watch over the little ones (some of whom were only aged four years) when they had an afternoon rest. The children usually had their baths after rest-time; these were organised in several zinc bath tubs arranged in one large room, and was most enjoyable! However, there were annoying days when I was not well, with the same trouble as before; Mother arranged for me to see doctors, but disappointingly no-one yet could find the root cause.

The Emergency was a difficult period for Miss Griff. There was a very worrying time when the communist terrorists surrounded the school, and the school was then put under armed guard. There were other concerns too; tigers were quite often seen in the vicinity!

At the start and end of the school terms the children would travel to and from their parents, having to negotiate the Highlands' forty miles of twisty roads and, due to the Emergency, they had to go by the armoured vehicles used for transporting the troops. This was essential for their safety, and in the plains these trucks could become extremely hot. They would have to join a convoy which was accompanied by armed forces and could only drive at the pace of the slowest vehicle. Bandits would try to ambush travellers in order to obtain provisions or currency and were often quite desperate, hence the necessity for armed protection.

Mother became friends with officers in the Gordon Highlanders who had just arrived in their new posting in the Cameron Highlands. She soon discovered that they loved Scottish dancing and were willing to teach anyone who was interested. Swiftly she organised an enthusiastic group to join us at 'Mar Lodge', where there was a lovely sitting room big enough for two eight-some reels! Our teachers were wonderfully patient with us, and as we began to make progress on these weekly gatherings, we all felt more confident and enjoyed these evenings tremendously. These young men would sometimes bring their bagpipes and obviously appreciated their evenings off-duty in a civilian house very much indeed.

We were rather excited one evening to hear that on his visit to Cameron Highlands, the Sultan of Pahang requested to come and see the Scottish dancing take place! This was such an honour! We all did our very best and he seemed to enjoy the evening very much. We usually had a break halfway through the time, offering coffee, tea or other drinks. He was intrigued by the instant Nescafe coffee, which was quite new those days, and asked if he could try some; naturally he was given a hot coffee at once, and he graciously said how much he liked it!

The Cameron Highlands Hotel, on the other side of the golf course from Mar Lodge, was hardly used because of the Emergency troubles, so it was decided to turn it into the school for students learning Cantonese. Every six months there would be a fresh intake of these students, and the residents on the Hill would be invited to meet them at various parties. Mother always hoped for more Scottish dancers, and Father would be delighted to find new golf partners or tennis players. We got to know several of the students and their wives and families. After a while, ballroom dances were arranged at the hotel and everyone would be invited. I thoroughly enjoyed these occasions too and, amongst others, met a very nice young man, David Stevens, a New Zealander, who became a regular visitor at Mar Lodge. He began to teach me to drive as Mother and I soon realised it was far too nerve-racking for us both when she did her best to teach me, and quite simply it was out of the question with Father! But, although we persevered, actually David did not inspire much confidence. It takes great skill to teach someone to drive, as I found out many years later with my own daughters! However, David and I tried a bit of golf and certainly enjoyed many picnics and walks and got on happily. It was a little embarrassing when I discovered he was getting very fond of me, and I realised, though I liked him as a friend very much, I just could not reciprocate his feelings.

Having completed his Cantonese course, David continued in the police force to take a post in Seremban and, eventually, happily married a girl from New Zealand, June, whom I met several years later.

Mother and I decided a little holiday would be a good idea, so we booked a chalet on the beach at Port Dickson and were very much looking forward to this; however, Father did not think he would be able to come. It must have been nearly two hundred miles to drive, and we were progressing well until, all of a sudden, we had a puncture! We realised we were in quite a remote place with jungle all around and were aware of possible lurking dangers from bandits. So we prayed earnestly but were dismayed that no one stopped to help us, all the traffic continuing swiftly on their way, seemingly oblivious to our plight! However, at last, a car did stop, and much to our relief two strong young men jumped out and offered help! They had American accents and briskly started to try to change the punctured wheel, only to find that none of us had a jack that would function. They were very resourceful and calmly removing large piles of Bibles from their boot, used these to lift the car to the necessary height for the wheel change! We thought this was wonderful and could not thank them enough! They explained that they were missionaries on the way to a meeting and that of course they were delighted to be able to assist us and to be the answer to our prayers!

We had a marvellous time at Port Dickson and then returned home to the Cameron Highlands, joining the 4 pm convoy near Tapah for the escorted drive up the dangerous road full of hairpin bends. It was a long climb, the slowest overladen vehicle holding everyone up rather painfully. Suddenly, about half way up the hills, there were urgent commands from our armed guard to stop, get out of the vehicles and take shelter as near to the mountainside as possible. We heard gunfire, numerous shots and loud commands, all rather nerve-racking as we did not know what was going on. After what seemed a long time, we were allowed to return to our transport, and, thankfully, to proceed with care. Eventually, really late, we arrived at our destination to find Father looking pale and anxiously awaiting our delayed arrival, having heard of our incident with bandits. This brought home to us again the reality of the Emergency.

Then there was new intake of students and a party to meet them on 4th February, 1952 at The White House, another delightful house which, like Mar Lodge, overlooked the golf course. Many of our friends were there, including Hester Todd who excitedly told me that her brother-in-law, Hugh Cassidy, was among the new students, much to her surprise! She introduced me to him, as did the hosts of the party, and she also introduced Hugh to Father, who was particularly interested because he remembered meeting Hugh as a little baby, when he had accompanied his father during a typhoon, up to the Peak in Hong Kong, many years before!

Hugh had recently volunteered to transfer from the Nigerian Colonial Service to Malaya because extra staff was urgently required due to the Emergency. Originally when he had joined the Colonial Service he had been asked where he would like to serve; his reply was, "First Hong Kong and then Malaya," but he was immediately sent to Nigeria! Although he grew to love Nigeria and its people, he was very glad to be able to make this transfer to the Far East, his real choice. He found learning to speak Malay was difficult for him, as it is so similar to the two Nigerian languages that he had had to learn previously – Hausa and Fulani – so it was decided that he should attend the two-year course to study Cantonese. This suited him well and he managed this enthusiastically!

Father promptly invited him to play golf with him, an invitation which he was delighted to accept, and Hester, his sister-in-law, happily made plans to meet him again too. Mother also invited him and several others to join our Scottish dancing, and we were all pleased that this plan seemed popular too. So Hugh and I met three times that evening – on his mother's birthday, as I later discovered!

Life continued at the bank for Father, and his tennis and golf whenever possible; bird-watching with a particular friend for Mother, entertaining and taking a special interest in the often rather lonely wives of the students; and Tanglin School for me. Hugh enjoyed playing golf with Father and came to our Scottish dancing evenings, where he proved to be a good dancer; but gradually he and I went for delightful walks, and somehow as time went by less golf was played and more walks took place! Looking back, I am amazed at how well we got on and understood one another, how much we had in common and how quickly an easy relationship developed. Hugh had a great repertoire of stories and would have us all in fits of laughter, but he also had a serious deeply thinking side and I remember looking at him as he partnered me at a Scottish dance one evening and realised how completely I could trust him. It was very important to both of us that we were Christians, and we had many discussions about this. He also taught me to drive, and here he was a wonderful, confidence-inspiring teacher and we had such fun over it all. One of his best ideas was that I should follow in my parent's A40 car while he drove ahead with his Morris Minor and do whatever he did – stopping or reversing, three point turns, hand signals or whatever – and with no one beside me disapproving any noisy gear changes or other mistakes, I found I coped very much better! Of course, the driving conditions on the Cameron Highlands were ideal for this, with not much traffic and some quiet tracks to practise on, although much care was necessary on the hairpin bend roads around the steep hillsides.

The time came for me to take my driving test, which had to be in Ipoh, on the plains. This was really alarming; it is a very busy town with the streets packed full with bullock-carts, bicycles, trishaws, people and numerous dogs wandering all over the roads! However, all went well, even (much to my relief) the dreaded reversing round a left-hand corner. The local people obviously thought this was part of their entertainment and would watch learner drivers with excitement and interest, and sure enough there was a little crowd waiting to see mistakes with glee, but this new driver disappointed them!

Hugh and I began to do more and more together and fell deeply in love. One day, on the 1st May, when by the beautiful Jungle Pool waterfall, on one of our walks, he asked if I loved him enough to marry him, and suddenly I knew very clearly that I did. It was such a romantic setting, but more than that, it was wonderful to know so definitely that God's hand was upon us both and to see something of His Plan for us.

Later Hugh took Father to one side and asked formally for my hand in marriage! And Father agreed! However, what made all the difference to his consent was that he had known Hugh's parents, meeting them so long before in Hong Kong at the time of the raging typhoon! Liking him very much, Father realised that he could completely trust his daughter to this young man! Another factor in my parents' agreement to my marriage at such a young age was that they had had to wait ten years before they could marry and they did not want us to have to cope with such a very long engagement. Not that we knew when our wedding could place at that stage, as it was difficult to see far ahead just what our plans could be, with Hugh continuing his language studies in Macau from July that year.

Hugh wanted to buy me an engagement ring and decided to take me to Kuala Lumpur to find one! Father asked if we would be able to stay in the Hong Kong and Shanghai Bank' s manager's house for our visit, and this was kindly agreed, although the manager apologised that he would be away at that time. However, Hugh and I had the pleasure of driving off together, first having to join the guarded convoy of vehicles down the forty miles of twisty roads, and then travelling on by ourselves happily to KL, as it was always known, to the lovely old-fashioned house that I remembered from my childhood. This house was where Mother and my sister had enjoyed that incredible hospitality when escaping from the Japanese invasion and from which came my vivid memory of playing at the bottom of the staircase saying the new word which had just come to me – 'beloved' – again and again; the feeling of being utterly at peace returned to me.

It was lovely being with Hugh and having the joy of finding my beautiful emerald and diamond ring and, as he slipped it onto my finger, realising with deep thankfulness and joy how much I really 'belonged' to him! We had a party to celebrate our engagement on our return, another great memory!

Hugh and Patricia (1952)

We did not have mobile phones, of course, in those days, but we had fun making signals to each other using a system of towels hung out on the balconies of our bedrooms, easily seen across the golf-course from Hugh's hotel to Mar Lodge! Shall we go for a walk? a drive? play golf? have a picnic? – with the corresponding answers! This was a useful way of communication, but one day I used the telephone urgently; Mother and I had found a bright yellow snake on our verandah and were terrified! Hugh valiantly hurried to our rescue in his car, brandishing a large pair of scissors with which, in a very clever way, he dispatched this frightening creature, much to our relief!

It was about this time I acquired a dog who needed a home. She was six months old, a pretty golden chestnut colour with a sweet temperament. Her name was Smudge, not a nice name for such an attractive dog, but as she knew it we all decided to keep to it. She was a delightful and undemanding companion, being obedient and easily trained, and we all grew very fond of her.

Shortly after that, Hugh's parents were on their way to England having just retired from Hong Kong. It was planned that Hugh would join their ship in Singapore and travel with them as far as Penang where I would meet them. This worked out beautifully, and I was always very grateful that I had this wonderful opportunity to meet Mama and Papa, as we all called them, before our marriage, and felt then we knew each other a little bit.

By this time the head of the language school, Roland, who became a real friend, complained that Hugh was spending rather a lot of time elsewhere rather than on his studies; I think he may well have been right! He and his wife, Diana, had recently moved into our guest rooms at Mar Lodge with their adorable daughters, Rosamund and Auriole, and we got to know them all well. However, Hugh passed the necessary exams and then had to prepare to go on to Macau where he was to spend the last eighteen months of his course, Macau being an ideal place then. Very little English was spoken there, only Portuguese and of course Cantonese, making it easier to concentrate on the language. He was one of the last students to have this opportunity; after his group completed the first six months at the Cameron Highlands the school transferred to KL for the two-year course.

It was so painful to part from each other, and we were both very sad about it, particularly as we just did not know when we would be able to see one another again. We drove down to Singapore where he was to catch a ship to Hong Kong, taking his beloved Morris Minor with him. I flew back to Ipoh where my dear Mother met me and did her best to comfort me. Hugh and I would write to each other every day, and these letters meant a great deal to us both. It was so interesting to hear of his new life in Macau, his Chinese language teachers and the ones who taught him how to write characters; it sounded a great experience! He enjoyed being in touch with his relations in Hong Kong, his Aunt Eva Pearce (a sister of his mother's) and cousin John especially, and old friends of his parents on his visits to Hong Kong. Macau did not have much in the way of shops so he would catch a ferry overnight for some provisions and to meet up with his people, relaxing a bit before returning to the rather bleak flat he had at that time and working very hard at his studies.

Lindsey flew out to Malaya again on leaving school, and Mother and I joyfully met her plane in Ipoh. It was wonderful to see her again, but I think it was quite difficult for her that so much had happened for me during the past year. Our correspondence was always very much appreciated, but it just isn't the same as actually talking to one another and, naturally, there was a great deal to catch up on for both of us.

Lindsey soon started to enjoy the holidays with all the many activities going on and enjoyed the Scottish dancing evenings too. We planned a holiday at Port Dickson again, but Father was very involved with his work and thought it best not to join us. So Mother, Lindsey and I set out for the charming chalet we had booked, which was right on the beach. One day, to our horror, Mother trod on a hidden sea creature which poisoned her foot very badly, causing her agony. The only way to deal this was to dash to the nearest hospital; thankfully I had my driving license by then, and with Lindsey taking wonderful care of Mother all ended well – but it certainly made us aware of dangers in the sea!

My parents were beginning to plan their retirement to England at the end of the year, so there were many things to consider. Lindsey had already been accepted to train as a nurse at King's College hospital on her return. Gradually it seemed that it may be possible for Hugh and me to marry before the family left Malaya. There was much discussion, letter-writing and decision-making. Hugh had his Cantonese exams at the beginning of January to fit in and was longing to marry me, so we started on definite plans for our wedding! The other question was where; there was no church in the Cameron Highlands, and the only other suitable venue seemed to be Malacca, where Hugh had been posted on his arrival in Malaya and which as a family we all knew!

It's alright now – God is in charge!

A wedding dress was ordered for me from England to match our beautiful old Brussels Lace veil, which so many of my family had worn. This fragile veil was sent to me, and to my joy the lovely embroidery anglaise wedding dress matched it perfectly! Lindsey sweetly agreed to be my maid of honour, and my dearly loved little friends Rosamund and Auriole were thrilled to be my bridesmaids. The Vicar of Christ Church, Malacca agreed to marry us – by special license because I was so young – and to our wonderment we found that he was Leslie Wilson, brother of Leonard Wilson the previous bishop of Singapore with whom we had had such fun sailing in 1948! The decision was made: 17th January, 1953 was to be our wedding day!

It was an amazing time for us all with so much to do and organise before the wedding and my parent's retirement. Somehow everything was accomplished in time: invitations to friends sent; passages on ships booked; the shopping, the packing, preparations; the farewell parties; finding new owners for Smudge; and, lastly, the organising of the beautiful flowers which were to be sent as a gift from Cameron Highlands to Malacca for the church service! Hugh also was busy with his exams and the plans for us to have a house to move into on our marriage in a new and lovely area of Macau!

A new life was about to start for us both, a whole new experience, and we were glad that we could commit every detail of it to our loving God!

CHAPTER TWENTY

Marriage

Our wedding day was wonderful! Hugh had arrived, a couple of days beforehand, from Macau, and it was an incredible joy to be reunited! The church was looking beautiful with the flowers from Cameron Highlands arranged artistically by Mother and Lindsey; my little bridesmaids came from Kuala Lumpur with their parents and, with Lindsey, were enchanting in all their pretty dresses; I felt very well supported. Father gave me away so lovingly, and words can't describe how I felt when I saw Hugh waiting at the chancel steps for me! It was a truly memorable wedding service! Hugh and I had had a very helpful meeting with Leslie Wilson earlier, and when it came to his homily during the service he spoke only to Hugh and me, inviting us to walk through the chancel to the altar steps together and then reminding us that we had just had our first walk together with God!

The reception was held at the Malacca Hong Kong and Shanghai Bank's manager's lovely house, and although not many of our friends had managed to come, due to the distances and dangerous roads at this time of the Emergency, it was a delightful occasion and very much appreciated.

On the way to Singapore, Hugh and I began our honeymoon in the Muar Hong Kong and Shanghai Bank house – how very kind all these dear bank managers were to us always! In Singapore we stayed at a delightful Government Rest House on the seashore at Changi. On the day that Father, Mother and Lindsey were to sail on the P&O Ship 'Carthage', for their return to England, we hurried to the docks at Singapore to say our goodbyes. This was a strange experience for me, with very mixed feelings: sadness, knowing I would not be seeing any of them for at least a couple of years; and yet, happiness with Hugh! After the ship's departure Hugh and I went to St Andrew's Cathedral in time for the short Evensong Service, and this was wonderfully comforting.

We sailed a few days later on the Blue Funnel ship 'Automedan' for Hong Kong and a completely new life for me! It was winter in Hong Kong and it seemed so cold after the Malayan heat, but I was thrilled with the sheer beauty of it all, loving the wonderful drive to Repulse Bay, where we were to continue our honeymoon in a fantastic hotel. I really enjoyed the many exciting places to which Hugh took me on all parts of the island. We gave a party for Hugh's relations so that I could meet them all, and they in turn returned hospitality to us in a variety of ways. One such party, I remember, seemed rather alarming! It was so very formal with the most beautiful table settings, each with numerous glasses and silver tableware. There were several courses of exotic dishes, and, as a new bride, I was served first each time, having to work out quickly how best to do this correctly without spoiling the elaborate decorations! It was a new experience, so different from the less sophisticated Malayan ways to which I was accustomed!

Then we had the joy of going to Macau – and our first home! This little house was delightfully situated on a hillside with a beautiful view from upstairs of the sea and the attractive Chinese junks sailing out to their fishing grounds. We had a little garden, and we were thrilled with it all! I loved turning this into a real home for us both, and although it was furnished, I enjoyed finding the small touches that make a real difference, such as pretty little lamps, putting up pictures on the walls and buying beautiful flowers, often gladiolas or poinsettias. Two very pleasant amahs helped in the house (it was important to offer work to people who so needed it in those days) and, as Hugh returned to his studies, we soon settled down to our new life together. Hugh's Chinese tutors would come to the house for one-to-one teaching, and I thought he was getting on very well with this tonal language and the Chinese characters. However, as our amahs did not speak any English, of course, I had to learn some Cantonese too! Hugh would write down phonetically what I needed to say with little signs to indicate the intonation; the amahs would eagerly help me and we all would have much laughter over my attempts – which were sometimes quite successful!

We loved seeing the old St Paul's Cathedral again when we visited Macau at the time of our Ruby Wedding, 1993! Here Hugh is standing on the steps leading up to the Facade!

It's alright now – God is in charge!

I so enjoyed living in this small Portuguese colony of Macau. Some of the buildings were of Portuguese architecture, and I loved the old cobbled streets, but most of all I admired the amazing facade of the old Cathedral left standing after a terrible fire. St Paul's Cathedral was first built in 1602 and then suffered a couple of destructive fires but was rebuilt each time until the last devastating one in the 18th century. It must have been a huge and magnificent building in its prime.

Hugh and I went to a little Chinese church on Sundays where everyone spoke Cantonese. We sang familiar hymns in English while the congregation enjoyed their Chinese version! The dear pastor would administer the Holy Communion to me in English – this loving gesture touched me greatly. We got to know a few of the friendly folk, but sadly the language was a real barrier to me; however, we did get to know a lovely elderly English couple who were missionaries in the past and whom I loved to visit. They gave me a miniature set of the gospels kept in a tiny basket, which I still have as one of my little treasures!

It was good to meet the other students on the Cantonese course, some of whom still keep in touch. Occasionally we would all join in with the local activities; there was one particularly outstanding Dance we all thoroughly enjoyed, for which we all had such fun dressing up and entering into the gaiety of the Macau Carnival.

Hugh and I were wonderfully happy and felt that 'no two people had ever been so in love', as we used to sing joyfully, using the words of a Danny Kaye song! I had had no idea how much one could be in love and be so completely happy! I know this was a wonderful blessing that we deeply appreciated.

Every three or four weeks we used to take the ferry across to Hong Kong for shopping and to meet some of Hugh's relations. This was always a pleasure; we would sail overnight, arriving at our destination early the following morning.[43] Hugh still kept his Morris Minor in Hong Kong, which was so useful to us. We sometimes stayed with John Pearce in his attractive apartment in Repulse Bay and also with Gordon Dunnett, in Kowloon, and it was lovely to get to know these cousins of Hugh's.

---

[43] Nowadays the crossing by the new fast ferries only takes an hour!

Then I began to suffer severe pain. Seeing a doctor in Hong Kong, I was carefully examined and this time was diagnosed with having a large ovarian cyst. Arrangements were made for an operation, which took place in Queen Mary's Hospital. When on the operating table I was given an epidural injection and told I would not feel any pain and could be able to watch the proceedings; however, when the surgeon started to pick up a knife I suddenly knew absolutely clearly that I did not want to see anything at all! Pity was taken on me and, mercifully, I was given another injection and slept soundly through the whole affair!

Hugh was with me as I was coming round and was alarmed when he noticed I was turning a peculiar blue colour; he hurriedly called for a nurse, with immediate results of resuscitation and life-giving oxygen! He was sure he had saved my life!

It was comforting to discover that the trouble I had coped with for several years was this very large ovarian cyst which, at times, must have leaked some fluid which acted like a poison causing me to feel so ill. In spite of a huge scar from the removal of the cyst I soon recovered and never again had the horrible symptoms that had caused me such distress for so long.

The Bishop of Hong Kong, Bishop R O Hall, kindly lent us his cottage on the Kowloon mainland near Shatin for a little holiday. This was delightful! This area now has a famous racecourse but was then in beautiful and unspoiled countryside. Many years later I found that this bishop was great friends with Leonard Wilson, who had become Bishop of Singapore. Bishop Hall was the first to ordain a woman as priest; this was in Macau, a part of his diocese, during the War and caused strong disapproval in the UK, in spite of the fact that he was such an outstanding and courageous Christian leader in Hong Kong.

Soon, to our great joy, I found that I was pregnant, and returning to my doctor this was confirmed; we were to expect our baby to arrive the following April. Life went on as normally as possible, and once morning sickness was not so troublesome, I kept very well. Hugh had always gone for a run on his own, early every morning before his studies, but we both continued to enjoy our walks, entertaining and also sometimes sailing in the harbour in Macau.

It's alright now – God is in charge!

Bishop Hall stayed with us over Christmas that year, visiting his little Anglican Church in Macau. This gave rise to another memorable time when the remaining students got together to plan the midnight service of Nine Lessons for Christmas Eve, each of us taking a reading! On returning to our house the Bishop noticed a Christmas decoration of some bells hanging by the front door, and started to sing, "Ding-dong, merrily on high" with great joy! This is delightful to recall! He spent Christmas Day with us, which we felt was a real privilege.

Hugh, having successfully completed his exams at the end of his Cantonese course, was to start working in Malaya. We left our dear little home in Macau where we had been wonderfully happy but knew the next phase of our life was about to begin. We realised gratefully that our Lord Jesus would continue to lead us. One of our lifelong habits was to pray together each evening, and we believe this was one of the things which helped us in a lovely marriage. We always found this a time when we could say sorry for everything necessary and tried to make good communication an essential part of our lives. So we confidently returned to Malaya – and another new stage in our lives!

On arriving at Singapore we drove in the Morris Minor to Kuala Lumpur, taking a route that had been advised as being 'safer' from the communist terrorists. We stayed at the Station Hotel, an ornate building I remembered from my childhood. It seemed wonderful to be back in this dear and familiar country, and although I had loved the buzz of Hong Kong, I found I much preferred the less materialistic and simpler way of life in Malaya!

Hugh found that his new post was to be the Chinese Affairs Officer for the State of Pahang, stationed at Bentong. After various preparations we set off for our new situation, first staying with the District Officer in Bentong before moving to our new home. To our delight, this was a typical Malayan house: a bungalow on sturdy brick stilts with wide verandahs outside all the rooms. There was a sweet little garden in the front in which, to my amazement, we found pink roses growing! The jungle pressed right up to the back fence, and there were a few other houses spaced out on either side of ours. We had a lovely view overlooking a valley and the little town of Bentong, with beautiful mountains beyond.

Hugh setting off to work from our home in Bentong, Pahang

Hugh would set off for his work early while it was still cool, driving the Morris Minor with its soft top down and putting it up later for necessary shade. He so enjoyed being able to use his Cantonese and would visit interesting places, meeting many different people in the course of his day. He even liked making speeches in Chinese, and I think this went down very well! However, as he did quite a lot of travelling all over the State of Pahang, he would sometimes be away for a few days, and there were occasions when he could not tell me his programme because of the terrorist situation. Everyone still had to be very aware of the Emergency and take precautions. There were few places where he would have felt it safe to use a phone, so at times I did not know where he was and tried very hard not to worry, realising that the little car with its soft top did not offer much protection should there be an incident! I learnt to pray hard in these circumstances and was always so relieved when he came safely home!

We settled down into new routines, employing a young man known as 'The Boy' to cook for us, and an amah to do the washing and house work. Again it was important to give local people work, and I believe we all appreciated each other!

As in all of the houses, cooking was done by wood-burning stoves, and the kitchens could become overpoweringly hot. There was never any air-conditioning, and while the ceiling fans would circulate the warm air, it was difficult to feel comfortable in the tropical heat at times, and I felt this even more in my pregnancy! There was a useful shop in the little town which would deliver necessities, and in spite of there being very few other shops we always seemed to manage all right! We were blissfully happy and I loved preparing for our baby, knitting little bootees and sewing little garments, even doing some attractive smocking on some of them. I had an old-fashioned Singer sewing machine and liked using this, setting it up in the baby's room. We managed to get a sturdy cot made and later a playpen and I began to feel more equipped; but there were no other European mothers with babies in Bentong at that time and nothing like clinics of any sort to help a new mother, so I just had to learn all I could as well as possible.

We got to know a St John's Ambulance worker, Barbara, who lived near us and who became an invaluable friend, teaching me and encouraging me always in so many ways – I was so grateful to her! She would take me with her sometimes, visiting little villages right out in the country or even in jungle settlements (in the 'ulu') where she would set up a clinic for people with all kinds of dreadful medical conditions. We were at such a place once when there was some sort of celebration going on with dancers and fire-walking; this was fascinating!

We decided that it would be best for me to have our baby in Kuala Lipis, where there was a small hospital. This was about sixty miles from Bentong and still in Pahang State. Kuala Lumpur with its much bigger hospital was in another state, Selangor, and would have been more difficult for Hugh to visit me, with dangerous roads en route with possible bandit activities.

A wonderful couple gave me hospitality in Kuala Lipis while I waited for our baby, who was born nearly a fortnight later than predicted. It was a great relief when, at last, it was time for me to go to hospital. It was the Easter weekend, and Hugh was there to take me. In those days husbands rarely stayed with their wives, so I was extremely grateful to a lovely Malay nurse who sat with me for the whole time of labour. I did not speak much Malay and she had no English, but somehow we communicated! I might have managed better if she was Chinese, perhaps! When the birth was imminent she called for the Matron. Matron was not all pleased to have to come just then – she was at a party! She was rather drunk and very cross, and particularly so when she found that the baby was to be a breech birth! Then she was very upset and told me indignantly that the cord was around the little one's neck. I suggested we prayed and this did not please her, but of course I did pray and thankfully all was wonderfully well! The doctor, also at the party, was too drunk to come at all!

I was absolutely thrilled with our beautiful little daughter and longed for Hugh to see her too! Eventually he came, rather subdued and quiet, thinking I would be as fragile as I had been after my operation, and then was delighted to see how well and happy I was and was overwhelmed with relief and joy at the safe arrival of his eldest daughter. We decided to name her Sheila, and we loved being together just adoring her! She weighed 8lbs and was a healthy colour, and she was the first European baby to be born at that hospital for many years. The other newborn little Indian and Malay babies were so petite and so beautiful with their dark skin and luxuriant hair, and somehow I don't think my large, rather pink baby was quite so attractive in their mothers' eyes!

Hugh then had to return to work and could not come to see me for several days, but my dear hosts came to visit me and (very exciting to me) Lady Templar, who was in Kuala Lipis for a formal visit with her husband, Sir Gerald Templar. Lady Templar was so sweet in her motherly way, in admiring Sheila and the little smocked garment I had made, and somehow that helped me because, of course, I so longed for my mother to see her too!

It was wonderful to return to Bentong and get used to motherhood; here, again, I was very grateful to Barbara for her wise advice! So life went on happily; we had several guests to stay, as always, and it was lovely for us to show off our precious baby to them!

I did have a most alarming scare once when I saw a dangerous snake in the bathroom, a krite, and, in a bit of a panic, called The Boy to help. He was marvellous and managed to get it out of the bathroom and through the door into the garden, where it leapt about menacingly until he killed it! It made me aware that it could have got into my darling little girl's cot, and I took huge precautions to make sure that her mosquito net 'shield' was always securely fastened.

It's alright now – God is in charge!

There was no church in Bentong; we wanted Sheila to be christened, so Hugh and I decided that we would take some leave and visit a great friend in Singapore, John Litton, who was to become her godfather. Her other godfather, Bill Baker, also joined us, but this was not possible for either of her godmothers, my sister Lindsey or Hester Todd, as they were both in the UK. The christening took place at St Andrew's Cathedral and it was a very special event!

Hugh making a speech in Cantonese

The time soon came for us to return to England for Home Leave. It was wonderful that we had come through our time in Bentong unscathed in any way, and we felt there was so much for which to thank God. Hugh was to have been posted to Tanjong Malim at one point, and the man who took his place was killed by the communist terrorists – this again made us realise the dangers we were all in during the Emergency.

We sailed on a P&O ship, the 'Canton', and after sailing through the Suez Canal we encountered very rough seas in the Mediterranean. There both Sheila (then aged nine months) and I were seasick! We arrived in England in February to find the first snowfall and freezing weather – a bit of a shock to us all! But it was so wonderful to see our families again and experience their joy of meeting little Sheila too.

We enjoyed this six months' leave tremendously and appreciated the different seasons so much after the tropics; winter, spring and summer were each marvellous in their varied ways. It was great to see how our parents had all settled into their new lives of retirement and were happy in their homes, each taking such an interest in their gardens and in their new lives. Sheila was growing rapidly and started walking and, as the whole family agreed, was a very special toddler!

Our return to Malaya was due again; this time our voyage to the Far East was on the Dutch ship the 'Oranje', and the next very pleasant three weeks seemed to pass so quickly on this luxurious liner. On disembarking at Singapore, we heard that we were to proceed at once to Kuala Lumpur where Hugh's next work was to be with the Public Service Commission.

CHAPTER TWENTY-ONE

Kuala Lumpur

Kuala Lumpur was to be our home for the next three years. We stayed at the Majestic Hotel to begin with, before moving to The Chalets, which were the temporary homes for the Malayan civil servants until a house became vacant. There were several of these little two-bedroom bungalows, each having a pleasant little verandah; this accommodation was quite adequate for a short spell, we all agreed! There was a large communal dining room in a separate building shared by us all.

By now Hugh realised that Malaya was to become independent sooner than anyone had expected and that he would need to find a new career. He had hoped to read law at University but WWII had put an end to his plans, so now he felt this would be an ideal opportunity to follow his dreams and become a lawyer! He started a correspondence course to read for the Bar and began to work very hard for this every day, before and after his usual day's work.

Little Sheila was a great joy to us, and we marvelled at the way she started talking; sometimes we were amused and at other times amazed. On Christmas Day she suddenly greeted us with "Happy Christmas!" She must have heard us say this, but it gave us such pleasure! And a little later when a tradesman came to sell vegetables, not knowing the word 'vegetable', she thought for a moment and explained that he had come about "eating-leaves"!

We found again to our great joy that I was pregnant and that the new baby was due the following June. At about this time we were able to move into our allocated house on Spooner Road. My first impression was of a large bungalow with big rooms, very high ceilings and with (it seemed) acres of floor – which had to be polished! While not having verandahs as such, all the rooms had expanded metal diamond-shaped 'netting' over the wooden louvered 'wall' surrounds, making these look as if they were verandahs. We learnt that the bungalow was on a 'monkey run', a route used by wild monkeys, and that this metal netting was to keep them firmly out! The house was on a slope and had deep, wide monsoon drains around three sides; it was built on brick pillars at the front to fit in with the lie of the land surrounding it. There was a pleasant garden with lawns and a huge tree giving shade.

It was wonderful to be in a house again after the rather hot little chalet! We found two very pleasant amahs to help us, Ah Heung and Ah Chan, whom I found essential with the work involved – polishing floors, the cooking with the wood-burning stove and extra help – as I was not well with the pregnancy. I became so fond of them and very much appreciated all they did for us.

Sheila loved the space of the house and garden and settled in happily. Hugh enjoyed his work first with the Public Services Commission and then, later on, with the Elections Commission. As his first new office was quite nearby, he liked to walk to it early in the morning. However he also continued to work very hard at his Bar exams. Sometimes I tried to help in the evenings with questions for him in preparation for the exams but am ashamed to say that I was often exhausted by then and would fall asleep!

Hugh's dear parents planned to visit us on their way back to England after a holiday in Hong Kong, and this was lovely for us all. Mama, looking at me, exclaimed with surprise that, at three months pregnant, surely the baby was due earlier than June as I seemed rather large already! Papa asked me earnestly to make this baby a boy; there was no one yet to carry on the name 'Cassidy'! But I did not think that was in my powers and quietly knew this baby was extremely precious whatever the gender!

My Malay doctor also began to tell me that I must have got my dates wrong! I asked if he thought I could be expecting twins, but as he knew I was a twin he firmly told me that twins never have twin births! I began to doubt him, and eventually he allowed me to have an x-ray six weeks before I believed the birth was due (no scans in those days, of course). As I waited for the result, the hospital Sister came to see me, and I rose politely to greet her. "Please sit down, Mrs Cassidy!" she said urgently. "Oh!" I said, "Am I having triplets?" She assured me that I was carrying just two babies! I was thrilled to bits! And then I wondered how I would cope with three little ones, Sheila being just about two years old at that point; and what about all the extra equipment, and another cot... All these thoughts rushed through my mind. We were not at all well-off; finances were very tight in those days.

But, wonderfully, friends were so supportive! Helga Jones gave us a cot that their son, Christopher, had outgrown, and gradually we assembled everything necessary and I began to feel more prepared! As I had not been well in the past months, I had not been able to make many new friends in Kuala Lumpur and was so grateful to those who lovingly provided for us in several ways.

Our babies decided to arrive a whole day later than my predicted date. Our lovely friends, Helga and Glen, took Sheila to stay with them and their little boy, Christopher, already a great friend of Sheila's. Hugh drove me to Bungsar Hospital, and within a few hours of having the most incredible attention from the hospital staff, who had not had a multiple birth for many years, our twins were born – identical girls! They weighed roughly 7lbs each, and were healthy and strong. I was so grateful, so awed and delighted, apprehensive and overwhelmed all at once! Hugh came as soon as he could to admire his new babies and to learn who was who, naming one little girl Anna, while I named the other little one Frances!

Neither Frances' godfather, Richard Cassidy, or her godmother, Mary, were able to be at the christening, but Helga was able to be with us, as was Anna's godfather, Stuart, and her godmothers, Diana and Christine. Christine lent us her family christening robe, and Frances (being the older twin) wore our family one.

Sheila proved to be a very loving older sister and very much enjoyed helping me with them! She seemed to have a natural aptitude for caring for babies, little children and many people with disabilities from a very early age.

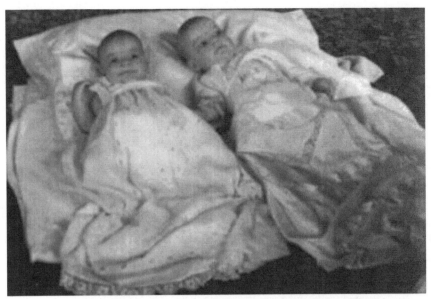

Frances and Anna on their Christening Day

*Hugh, Sheila (aged 2½) and Patsy in the garden
at 2 Spooner Road, K. L.*

Our twins were lively little babies even before they were born and
were always so energetic, crawling at six months old, climbing soon

afterwards, and walking confidently quite soon too; they were real 'handfuls'! They used to enjoy climbing up the expanded metal netting surrounding the rooms, the diamond shapes being just the right size for their hands and feet! This netting was useful too in keeping *our* little 'monkeys' safely indoors! I used to come into the rooms sometimes, gasping at their agility – and with dismay, wondering who to rescue first from the ceiling height!

Later we found it was wise to put Sheila into the large playpen for undisturbed peace with her dolls, books and crayons while her sisters had fun round about! And they *were* fun, with a lively sense of humour – and very cuddly! Sheila had never been so adventurous, and I think I was quite spoilt with her totally different temperament! However, they were three happy little people, and we found we enjoyed them all so much in their very differing ways in spite of worrying moments!

One of my great concerns for Frances and Anna was that they might fall into the deep monsoon drains around the house, and also that they could actually explore between the low pillars underneath the house, with me wondering anxiously what nasties lurked there! Another problem was the wild monkeys, which came periodically using their familiar route over the roof of the house, leaping down into the garden, climbing the large tree and generally feeling free to explore everywhere! Sheila remembers the hairy hand of a monkey taking a banana from a dish too near an opening for a window fastening; we soon learnt to be more careful! But we never knew when these monkeys might visit and had to hurry the children into the house safely; monkeys can be quite dangerous at times.

I often longed for family to be there with us to admire my little daughters and to love them! In some ways this was a very lonely time for me; Hugh was working very hard in the office and also preparing for his impending exams. At first it was difficult for me to manage to go anywhere by car with the three little girls. There were no proper car seats for small children in those days, and I found taking two carry-cots in an ordinary car and making sure Sheila was safe could be daunting! I would have loved to have been able to visit friends and to enjoy seeing their children too, and even to have a change of scenery. I think I felt rather trapped at times, and now wonder if I had some postnatal depression.

Later on I had a vivid dream; my gleeful little twins were jumping about on top of our huge dining table, and I just could not catch them. I felt in despair and in a very dark place. In my dream I suddenly saw that a bright light was shining from under a door, and when I opened it I saw Jesus was sitting peacefully in an armchair in this room! He beckoned to me to come to Him, and as I knelt before Him, He gently encouraged me to tell Him exactly what was distressing me. Even though He knew everything, He wanted me to express every detail! His love and compassion was marvellous! This was a wonderful and memorable experience, and very healing. There had been no one else with whom I could really share what was happening and how inadequate I was feeling, and I am not even sure that I had fully realised this myself!

I remember asking myself what my grandmother would do in my circumstances, and clearly thinking she would read right through the Bible! So I started at Genesis and eventually read all the way through, finding treasures in the words and particularly when I came to Jeremiah and read in chapter 29, verses 11-13, "'For I know the plans I have for you,' declares the Lord, 'plans to prosper you and not to harm you, plans to give you hope and a future. Then you will call upon me, and I will listen to you. You will seek me and find me when you seek me with all your heart. I will be found by you,' declares the Lord…" I felt that the Lord was actually promising me this and decided I would try to search for Him with all my heart! It was such an encouraging thought, and I have continued to do this ever since. I also tried to 'practise the presence of God' and realised I had great way to go! I loved the psalms and the wonderful truths of God's faithfulness and love; in fact, I began to find the Bible so exciting as well as challenging, but often very difficult to understand!

There were many other things I also enjoyed, particularly being asked to look after a Triumph sports car for a friend who was going back to England for his leave! I loved having opportunities to drive this little car! Being an open top it was not suitable for the children and, when Hugh was at home, I discovered that I liked going off on my own at times!

At the turn of a key
Feeling gloriously free
Acceleration! Exhilaration!

It's alright now – God is in charge!

Liberation – free to be me, just me!

I used to go to the market in the town about once a week, but usually this was with our Ford Zephyr; I would go very early before the children were up, just as it was getting light, while Hugh was studying for his law exams. I was fascinated by the huge variety of fruit and vegetables on display, the spices, the differing smells and also the fragrances from beautiful flowers. It was interesting to make choices and to come home with delicious fresh produce. Another routine early morning job was doing the washing with the help of our newly acquired washing machine. It was not fully automatic and I used to do all the rinsing in the bath. Everyone in the heat of the tropics would change all their clothes at least once a day, so there was always quite a lot of washing, besides the piles of terry-towelling nappies when the babies were very little – no disposable nappies then! I was most grateful to the amahs, who would do the ironing as well as the housework and cooking!

Hugh and I so enjoyed Sundays – when Hugh did not do any reading for his Law exams – and we loved the opportunity to be together for a whole day with our little daughters. When it was possible, Hugh and I used to go to St Mary's Church services, but usually this had to be separately as there were no facilities for babies (although later Sheila went to the little Sunday School). The Vicar then was Chiu Ban It, a wonderful man who became a very special friend of ours. Years afterwards, he was consecrated Bishop of Singapore. St Mary's Church was an attractive building situated at one end of the green, known as the Padang. Decades later this church became a cathedral and was dwarfed by huge new skyscrapers; like St Andrew's Cathedral in Singapore, it became almost unnoticeable when surrounded by such tall buildings!

Sheila started to go to a pleasant little nursery school run by the Catholic Church. I made her a white uniform with a pleated skirt and thought she looked so grown up and, with her curly hair, adorable too! The nuns were very impressed that she could read so well before she was four years old and were full of compliments! Sheila still remembers reading the books there.

I enjoyed making nearly all of the girls' clothes. I struggled at first with patterns and had a few disasters, but I loved finding pretty materials for their dresses. I thought it very important that Frances and Anna were not dressed alike and later encouraged them to have quite different hairstyles. They were unique individuals, even though they both did seem to like the same sort of activities! At first it sounded as if they even had their own little language, which Sheila used to interpret for Hugh and me very helpfully! Sheila always was a delightful companion to me, and we would have lovely chats, particularly at bedtime. She was so interested in many things and loved to explore ideas with me about nature and the stars and how God made the world.

We got to know some impressive blind people whom we admired very much, also attending St Mary's Church, and became good friends. I used to read all sorts of things to them which they then transposed into Braille as part of their work. This seemed a great skill to me! My daughters all still recall the picnics we used to have with them, taking them to attractive places nearby. Sheila had an amazing understanding of their blindness and would particularly look after Mary, leading her so confidently that Mary trusted her completely!

We also met some wonderful missionaries who worked in one of Gerald Templar's New Villages, Jin Jang, just outside K. L. I loved assisting in their clinic, leaving my little girls, as they grew older, with Ah Heung and Ah Chan. This also gave me an opportunity to use a little of my limited Cantonese! But one day when I returned home I found the amahs were a bit subdued and wondered why; almost immediately, however, a car turned up at the house and a lady emerged telling me with great concern that earlier she had "picked up two little men from Mars on the road, wearing nothing but a pair of amahs' wooden shoes between them!" She had heard that there were twins at this house and brought them here. I was really grateful but very shocked to hear that the amahs evidently had not watched over their young charges properly! Even though they both assured me this would never happen again, I was reluctant to ever leave my precious little girls under their care after this episode.

However, there was a 'flu epidemic at some point, and hearing of the seriousness of the situation and how much my help was needed, I decided that I would trust the amahs with Frances and Anna (Sheila was at her school) and, with their assurances, helped at the clinic with its huge numbers of suffering patients. Hugh was about to take an important Bar exam that morning but appeared to be quite ill, with a high temperature (possibly the 'flu); however, he very firmly insisted he would take the exam so I had to leave him to his decision. On arrival at the clinic, I asked my dear missionary friends to pray for him. We prayed together and then got on with the overcrowded clinic and a very busy morning. On returning home, I was relieved to find all was well with my children, and soon Hugh also came back, looking radiantly well! He told me how he had suddenly felt the fever leave him and that he was quite alright again. I told him about the prayer. And later we heard that he passed the exam with flying colours; there was much for which to praise God!

We used to love taking the children to the nearby Lake Club where there was an attractive swimming pool. Frances and Anna could swim before they could walk, mostly under the water, very confidently. Sheila had not had that opportunity so young and took a little longer to feel sure about it all.

Once when the babies were very small, I took Anna to change and heard that Sheila had spoken to someone who was admiring Frances, her little sister; pointing to the changing room, she had said, "There's more in there!" very proudly. The stranger was impressed and soon duly admired the other little one – very much admiring Sheila too!

One day I took Sheila and Frances to the changing rooms, only to return to find a worried looking husband holding Anna tightly. He explained he had lost sight of her momentarily and looking at the pool had spotted her sitting on the bottom with a big smile, apparently quite happy! He was horrified and plunged in to rescue his tiny daughter! We wondered if she would have just swum easily to the surface when she needed to draw breath – or not? It was an alarming experience for loving parents!

At one point, Hugh was due local leave and we were invited to stay with some friends, Gordon and Josephine, near Penang. This was a delightful visit and much appreciated; it was so good to meet these friends again. They lived right by the sea and naturally we all went down to the beach as soon as possible. To my horror, Frances and Anna, aged fourteen months, both walked straight into the sea with little waves breaking gently over their heads, showing no fear whatsoever and just loving it all! Admittedly it was a calm day and we were all there, poised to help if it was necessary, but their fearlessness was amazing!

There were other things I had to adjust to as well. There was a very good playground with swings and slides at our local park. The slides were of varying heights, the top of the steps of the tallest one was well out of my reach, and later my energetic pair loved to hurry up these metal steps and hurtle confidently down. They never did come to any harm, but how could I be sure of that?

By then our friends, Glen and Helga, who had had Smudge, our dog, for several years, were returning to England and gave her back to us, so walking to the park was a pleasant way to exercise a much loved dog and lively little children!

The situation in Malaya was changing rapidly, and there was more and more talk about the future. Independence of the Federation of Malaya from British colonial rule[44] was to be on 31st August, 1957. Once it became increasingly clear that the communist threat posed during the Malayan Emergency was petering out, agreement was reached on 8th February, 1956 for Malaya to gain independence from the British Empire. However, for various reasons it was decided that the official proclamation of independence would only be made the next year, on 31st August, 1957, at Stadium Merdeka in Kuala Lumpur.

Many civil servants were leaving Malaya as the great day approached; some people were offered another few years of work so that there would be a smooth transference of leadership, and this proved to be a real success. Hugh was offered the option to stay until 1960, but first he was due six months' Home Leave after completing his three-year tour of duty.

My sister, Lindsey, and her fiancé, John, were to be married on 29th November, 1958, in England, and we timed our leave to be earlier than usual in order to be there for this important occasion! Sheila, aged four-and-a-half, was to be a bridesmaid along with John's little niece, Jane, of the same age. Hugh also planned this leave so that he could eat the all-important 'dinners' that were still compulsory at the Inner Temple! However, leaving Malaya at this point meant that his successor gained the award for working at the Elections Commission that Hugh should have had!

---

[44] 'Merdeka', as it was known in Malay

It's alright now – God is in charge!

The planning, packing, storing all accomplished, and passages booked on a German ship, the 'Hamburg', we set sail again for England, anticipating a special leave!

CHAPTER TWENTY-TWO

New Life in England

Sailing on The Hamburg was a very pleasant experience, apart from one very scary moment! As a family we had adjacent cabins, each with a porthole and en suite facilities, and were delighted with our comfortable accommodation. There was a nursery on board this ship with helpful staff; this made such a difference as we travelled with Sheila, now four-and-a-half years, and our two-year-old twin daughters. They were all supervised while Hugh and I could enjoy the excellent meals in peace and luxury!

One evening at the girls' bedtime, when running water for their baths, I came into their cabin again and immediately noticed that Frances was nowhere to be seen. I asked Anna where she was, and she waved happily to the upper bunk by the porthole. To my utmost horror I saw that the porthole was wide open! Thoughts rushed through my mind. A cleaner must have left it open... What can one do to rescue a little child from the sea, and where would I find her if I jumped in after her? How could one stop this huge ship and get it to turn around? Prayers poured through me, and I felt quite faint with fear for my precious Frances! And then, to my unspeakable relief, there she was, just out of my sight behind the cabin door! It was a moment I will never forget!

We did remonstrate with the staff on duty, who were very apologetic and understanding and made sure that this porthole would never be left open again. But it made us even more aware of possible dangers. The exposed upper decks were lovely, but we realised that the rails surrounding them could be very tempting to little people who liked to explore and climb everything possible. Thankfully, however, there was plenty on board this ship for all the children to do, and our three soon made friends with the many other children. We were very glad of the little swimming pool too and spent much time in its vicinity, enjoying the warmth of the sun while we could. But as the Hamburg sailed further north there was a distinct chill in the November air. The girls were rather pleased with the warm clothes we had for them, and we all began to adjust to winter. When the ship called at Genoa, it was wet and cold and the girls remember that Hugh bought umbrellas for each of his family. They also remember him telling them about the Blue Peter flag and how it would be raised just before a ship sailed.

It was so wonderful to disembark and to be back in England once more. It was marvellous to experience the joy of close family and their lovely welcomes and delight over seeing Sheila again and meeting Frances and Anna for the first time. Then we had the pleasure of meeting John and being at home for some of the preparations for his marriage to Lindsey at the end of November.

My generous parents gave us the use of their delightful cottage on the river at Irstead on this leave – a magnificent gesture! And we loved them for that – and for their dear selves! They moved into the sweet little boathouse next door, where Hugh and I had stayed very happily on our previous leave.

The wedding at the little Irstead Church was so lovely; Lindsey looked beautiful, her John so handsome in his morning coat, and the bridesmaids were enchanting in their pretty pink dresses. Sheila remembers being carried carefully over a large puddle so it must have been wet, but it was a very special day and much enjoyed by us all.

Father had cleverly constructed a sandpit for the children and this was a great success, even on very cold, snowy days in the depths of winter. Anna remembers seeing snow for the first time and thinking there was sugar sprinkled thickly everywhere! I explained about snow and that it was very cold, and then, to our surprise again, we found how much all the girls loved it and that they would happily play in it for hours in their brightly coloured, warm, padded outfits. We were grateful too for the help with our daughters given by a young girl whom Mother had found, so we all began to settle down and feel at home. Sheila started going to the local school, a whole new experience for her. She seemed to take this in her stride and soon began to speak with a rich Norfolk accent! Once, when solemnly observing some ducks that Uncle John had just shot on the nearby marshes, she asked sadly if they had been killed because Uncle John did not like ducks... Her voice rising at the end of the sentence was so authentically Norfolk that it was hard not to be amused, but it was quite a difficult question to answer!

Hugh worked for his Law exams every day and was successful in keeping another three terms of the required 'eating dinners' at the Inner Temple in London. In the past these occasions would have been the main opportunity to discuss Law and to gain knowledge to pursue the career of a barrister. This Bar tradition dated back to the 13th century when it was necessary for students to eat eighteen formal dinners at the hall of their chosen inn to qualify at the Bar. Within this last decade this rule has been scrapped, and the old traditions have now been brought more up to the present century with modern lectures and debates, and a choice of different activities to continue their law studies at their inn, such as residential weekends and various evening lectures and meals. Formal dining in the hall is still possible, but 'eating dinners' as such is no longer compulsory! I admired Hugh very much indeed for his single-mindedness and determination over those last years as Malaya became independent, wisely thinking ahead about his coming retirement from the Malayan Civil Service in order to start a new career.

We began to consider where we would live when we finally returned to England and how to find a good school for our daughters. It was a relief to us that our girls would not have to go through the long separations from parents that Hugh and I had both suffered as children. Our friends Roland and Diana had settled in Kent and told us about the school their daughters, Rosamund and Auriole, attended. We discussed this at length and decided that their town seemed the best place for us to live too. It was within reasonable distance of both our parents and, very importantly, there was a good train service to London for Hugh, which he was bound to need for his work in the future. Roland and Diana were wonderful friends to us, and we were very grateful for their support and advice. Later they wrote to us about possible houses in suitable locations for commuting to London and then were so helpful in finding just the right flat for us to move into on our arrival back from Malaya.

After several idyllic months in England, it was time for us to return to Malaya for Hugh's last tour of duty. Being so lovingly supported by our dear families and friends had meant a great deal to us, but we realised it wouldn't be such a long parting this time and said our farewells quite cheerfully.

We knew that this voyage was to be on the German ship Hamburg again, and we boarded the familiar vessel with pleasure. To our surprise we found that there was a Hungarian circus travelling out to Japan! Stables had been built on the afterdeck for the seven black and seven white horses, and there were large cage-like enclosures for the tigers. This provided much interest for all us passengers! We were asked, however, not to go near the black horses as apparently they were trained not to be friendly, presumably for a particular act in the Big Top. After a couple of weeks, passengers were warned that the sugar lump supply was dwindling rapidly and we were asked, please, would we all stop feeding the white horses!

We proceeded straight to Kuala Lumpur as soon as we arrived in Singapore. By this time we had a small estate car, a green Hillman Husky, which became known as the Green Dragon and was ideal for our little family. We found much had changed in Malaya; many of our friends had already left, and there were problems in fitting personnel to the right work required. Hugh was given entirely new work again; this time he was to be the Financial Officer for the Sate of Perak and stationed in Ipoh!

We were allocated a very small chalet in Ipoh which was only just adequate and very hot. We started to make new friends and joined St John's Church in Ipoh where we both became quite involved, Hugh being asked to be the Church Treasurer and I to help in the Sunday School.

There was an outbreak of measles, and both Sheila and Anna became very ill. The doctor had just received some vaccine for the first time and, seeing how ill both these little girls were, asked us if we would like to try this for Frances as a preventative. We gratefully agreed – and Frances was fine! Otherwise we were all very well and enjoyed living in Ipoh. Sheila liked her small, privately run school, which was a very good one, and we felt very proud of her as she progressed rapidly! Smudge, our dog was returned to us, and we began to feel happily settled – until we discovered that Smudge was very shortly expecting puppies! Sadly, she became seriously ill and then was unable to feed her puppies. Discussing this with the vet we came to the terrible conclusion that it was kindest to put her and her poor ailing puppies to sleep. I was very distressed indeed!

It was a relief when a very nice modern house was offered to us in Tiger Lane, and we enjoyed moving in with the feeling that we could start again. We were happy to be asked if we could take a sweet little cat to look after – who was immediately called 'Tiger'! We were very thankful to have a Chinese cook and his wife to help us in the house and were delighted with the excellent meals produced. 'Cookie', as he liked to be called, could also bake very well and made beautiful birthday cakes for each of the girls in due course.

We found that we needed a second car, and bought a little second-hand Morris Minor, promptly named 'Emma'. This was necessary to take the children to their different schools, while Hugh had the other for his office, several miles away. Hugh was getting used to his new job even though he was not trained for it at all. He always took every opportunity to use his Cantonese but I think was quite sorry that with all that was happening in the Civil Service just then, life was becoming so different from his earlier expectations. However, he began to enjoy working with his new colleagues and met some very interesting people in the course of his work, including the Sultan of Perak.

Frances and Anna, now aged three, started at a little nursery school and really liked all the activities; there was a lot for them to do! One day, to their joy, they discovered some kittens in a room near the usual schoolroom; the teacher, Mrs Roberts, was horrified to find them playing with these tiny pets, but she paused to watch for a moment and told us afterwards that she had never seen such young children handle little kittens so gently and that they obviously had a wonderful way with animals!

We all enjoyed our daily visit to the Swimming Club, and the girls continued to improve their swimming skills enthusiastically. Then poor little Anna kept having infections and was not allowed into the pool; this was particularly hard on her as she loved swimming most of all. It was about this time I had fun making up stories for the girls at bedtime, always starting off with, "There was a little girl who had a little curl right in the middle of her forehead, and when she good she was very, very good, but when she was bad, she was horrid!" This led to all sorts of adventures that Lucy got involved with, helped by three eager little girls!

With Anna's continued tonsillitis it was decided that she should have a tonsillectomy, which was carried out at Batu Gajah Hospital. It was a surprisingly good experience, and she recovered quite quickly after that! Anna remembers the hospital room that she and I shared, being pleased when Hugh brought her sisters to visit her and how Frances was so excited by the little presents I had left them, a colourful toothbrush each, amongst other things! Anna felt quite envious of the new toothbrushes, although I am sure I would have given her presents too!

Hugh was due local leave, and we planned to go to Penang; this seemed ideal, especially for Anna to make a complete recovery. It was such a lovely holiday, seeing our friends Roy and Mary and their little boy Mervyn, and exploring the island, visiting beautiful beaches. Frances seemed to have extra liveliness and sense of fun and kept us all entertained. Frances will always remember a picnic when, having just peeled a banana, a monkey swiftly snatched it out of her hands, much to her indignation! Both Frances and Anna remember a train that "went up steps" with jungle all around; it took me a moment to work this out until I thought of the funicular railway up Penang Hill!

A dear Chinese couple, whom we had met before in Kuala Lumpur, now lived in Ipoh, and I loved to visit them. They were both blind, although Peter had a little sight in one eye and could make the most beautiful baskets. He cleverly made two woven cases to fit behind the Hillman Husky front seats, which we used for many years, and several other baskets which we later took back to England. Agnes was totally blind and expecting a baby. I was full of admiration for the amazingly skilful way she coped in her little house; seeing her lighting a fire, cooking over it and filling a thermos with boiling water remain as vivid memories! Christopher was safely born and we loved him too! Hugh had the honour of being invited to be his godfather. Our other Chinese friends from Kuala Lumpur visited us in Ipoh, and we always hoped to stay in contact with all these dear families (and have had the real joy of doing so ever since).

One day we planned to return to Cameron Highlands. Anna recalls how we told the children that there used to be 'bandits' near that road; it was the first time she had heard that word. It was marvellous for Hugh and me to show the girls the particular places we knew so well. We decided to have a picnic by the Jungle Pool and told them that this was where Dad had proposed to me – and was accepted! We were just enjoying our picnic lunch when a sudden downpour of heavy rain made us all scuttle under the picnic rug we had been sitting on and it kept us more or less dry! We then took our daughters to meet Miss Griff at Tanglin School and proudly introduced them to this remarkable lady, who was really sweet to us all. It was a very special day!

Both Frances and Anna recall how I took them to a rubber plantation near Tiger Lane and showed them how rubber was tapped. They also remember that Sheila told them it was alright to throw stones at the boys next door – and that they immediately did so! I did not know about this at that time! Had the boys been teasing them, I wonder? The twins respected Sheila very much and have reminded me how once, a couple of years later in England, they had all been out on bikes; Sheila wanted to go home, but they both were reluctant until she suggested that they look upwards to see large birds flying about and warned that such eagle-like birds could snatch little girls! This ruse worked well and they all came hurrying back!

Our time in Ipoh drew to a close in October, 1960, and we had to pack almost everything. With all the boxes, trunks and cases carefully marked and numbered, and the house emptied, we moved back to The Chalets. This time we were given the more generous accommodation upstairs in the main house, which was comfortable and pleasant. Hugh had much to do in handing over to his successor and was very busy indeed. Frances, particularly, continued to amuse us all with her great sense of humour and somehow added such a light-hearted air to everything.

Although several friends had already retired by now and returned to England, we still had many friends locally to say goodbye to. We embarked on our final voyage in Penang, on the small Danish ship 'Selandia'. This ship, unusually, had four masts and no funnel – "four stick bamboo, no puff-puff" as someone has amusingly described it! It seemed quite old-fashioned having been built in 1938, and I discovered later that it was scrapped a couple of years after our return in 1962. She was a cargo ship with four holds, carrying about sixty-four passengers and returning to Copenhagen. While it was a pleasant voyage, it was not so good for the few children on board, who were only permitted to play on one deck with just a little swing fixed to the 'ceiling' formed by the deck above. No sunshine penetrated this deck, and parents were 'on duty' at all times. Sheila made friends with another little girl of her age, and they amused themselves with puzzles, books or games, keeping themselves happily busy. There was one highlight each day when at lunchtime the children were allowed to use the small swimming pool; this was greatly appreciated! The Captain heard about Frances' and Anna's delight in this and often came to watch the little 'tadpoles' as he called them! Anna particularly amazed him with her confidence and how much she swam under water.

Hugh needed to take every opportunity to study for his final exams for the Bar – and disappeared to a sunny upper deck! While this was laudable and understandable, I was a bit envious of his sunshine at times! His correspondence course, while it had been excellent, was very demanding. He did so well to persevere with it over the last few years until it was completed.

The children enjoyed travelling through the Suez Canal and seeing camels walking along the eastern bank, which astonished them all – some of Noah's Ark's animals come to life! The Selandia docked for a while at Port Said, Cairo, when a 'gulli-gulli' man came on board to amaze us all with his magic and skill! He produced tiny chicks from his sleeve, or ear, and even from the children themselves! There were other ingenious moves too swiftly accomplished for the eye to follow; it was a wonderful and memorable entertainment!

The weather turned colder towards the end of October, and thankfully we were permitted to use an inside lounge for the final part of the journey. We disembarked at Dover and, as we watched the Selandia sail on towards her destination at Copenhagen, we realised with quite mixed feelings that this would be our last voyage. Hugh took the car, fully laden, to visit his parents in Virginia Water, while I went straight to Norfolk by train with the children to see my parents. What joyful reunions! We then hurried to Kent and our new home, as quickly as possible organising everything necessary, including the uniform for Sheila to start at her new school. The autumn term had already begun, and when Hugh and I met the pleasant school secretary we were rather chided for bringing our daughter so late for the new school term! We tried to explain we had only just arrived in England and that, of course, we needed to see our parents as a top priority. But we soon understood that this was an infringement of the law; Sheila should have been at school!

A whole new life was ahead of us all again. The flat so kindly arranged by Roland and Diana was very suitable as a first step towards our own home; it was within easy walking distance of the schools, shops and station, and we felt it was such an answer to our prayers... but I don't think I was prepared for what seemed a whole new culture and way of life.

Hugh and I both had to take the British driving test as our Malayan licenses were not valid here. We each nervously had a driving lesson beforehand, as it mattered very much to be able to drive in England. Anna recalls being in the back seat when I had my lesson and, being asked to be quiet, she realised this must be important! Hugh took his test first and passed. Mine was the following day with same instructor; he made me go on a completely different route from Hugh's. I knew the expression 'knees turning to jelly' and this is just what seemed to happen to me! However, most gratefully, I also passed; this was such a relief to us both.

We soon found a nursery school for Frances and Anna; no uniform was necessary so I found them each an attractive tartan skirt to be worn with different coloured jerseys. Anna later told that she did not like this school very much: "It was a dark building and rather gloomy. The teachers seemed strict but not in a nice way – officious somehow. There were rules: the children had to hang up their coats in a certain way and have a rest after lunch, sitting at tables with their heads resting uncomfortably on the table."

Before long Frances suddenly had chicken-pox! Soon Sheila and Anna succumbed and then so did I. Hugh was working very hard for his final exams. He decided as Frances was recovering that it was easiest to pop her back into bed in the room the girls shared and look after all three of them at the same time; this worked surprisingly well! But I was quite ill. Diana wonderfully came to our rescue when Hugh had to go to London to take his exams, and then my darling Aunt

Penny came to us from Norfolk to take care of us all. She also was splendid! It was nearly Christmas so normally I would be busy preparing for everything, but Penny did her best, even finding attractive Christmas wreaths and decorations – until she was taken quite seriously ill with an infection which turned into pneumonia. Our kind new doctor did all she could to help the stricken family, suggesting that Penny went to hospital, but Hugh and I felt we would much prefer to try to look after her ourselves, and somehow we did. It was a wonderful time in many ways, drawing us all much closer to one another with a great sense of being deeply blessed. We really missed this beloved aunt when she was well enough to return home to Norfolk.

The great day came at last when Hugh was called to the Bar! He had passed all his exams, and I was extremely proud of him and of all his hard work and achievements! Now he was ready to start a new career, so he looked and prayed in earnest for the right one. This was not easy at that time, but through a chance meeting with an old school friend he was offered a legal position in a firm, which later led on to working with BP Chemicals as a legal advisor.

On the first day of his new career, Hugh dressed in the customary dark suit and bowler hat and, carrying his brief case and black umbrella, walked to the station to catch the train to London. Ahead of him he saw a flock of sheep being carefully guided by the shepherd in charge to the local market, a flock of sheep each of which looked identical; then, suddenly, he saw what seemed to him a large flock of commuters, all dressed alike with dark suits, bowler hats and carrying briefcases and black umbrellas who, like him, were hurrying to catch a train to London!

On his return home that evening Hugh told about his interesting first day at the office, his new work and colleagues – and the game of cricket everyone played with rubbers and rulers in their lunch hour! He also told us about both the flocks of sheep he had seen and added thoughtfully that the Lord tells us that He is the Good Shepherd; he told us how the Good Shepherd loved and knew each of that crowd of men but also, unlike the sheep, how everyone would have the choice of whether to belong to this Good Shepherd or not. Hugh saw afresh how he had been wonderfully shepherded all his life. He felt so reassured and grateful again for his new work as a lawyer, knowing that his Good Shepherd was in charge of his life and family. But he also always remembered this flock of commuters with great amusement!

Another phase in our lives was beginning: a new career, new schools, even a new culture with such a different way of life. It was almost overwhelming at first, but I believe we learnt increasingly to trust that the Good Shepherd, the Lord our God, is in charge of whatever happens at every stage of our lives.

Looking back over many decades now, I am awed to see how wonderfully the Lord has always taken care of us, His sheep! For example, I read that at the time when we were fleeing from the Japanese a train from Penang and the north (and it most probably was ours) was ordered to return to the north. Everyone who had not got accommodation in Kuala Lumpur was told to get on board again, and the tragedy is that this train encountered the enemy and a great many people were killed. I have felt very sad about that and have thought much about those lovely nuns in our carriage; what happened to them? How was everyone else? This appalling news certainly made me appreciate our safe journey to Singapore all the more! As there was so little communication and trains were urgently needed for the movement of troops, railway lines had to be kept clear so it is likely that 'our' train was shunted into a siding somewhere as a temporary measure before being sent on its way again. We also heard, much later, that two or three babies were born on this train as a hospital had been evacuated, many people from further north had also been suddenly ordered to leave, this train had been fired on by enemy action, and there had been much panic and chaos. Penang and other towns had been bombed, and there was great confusion and chaos everywhere in Malaya.

Hugh's comment that it is our own choice whether or not to follow the Good Shepherd and become part of His Flock is true... I believe I have also found that this is a choice to be made over and over. We can belong to the Flock, but sometimes can wander off and get 'lost'. I can be disobedient and choose not to be loving and forgiving, or I can ask for forgivingness and return to the safety of the sheepfold. I believe being secure within the Flock is a great privilege; to know the security of God's love is wonderful beyond words. I also believe that learning to trust is a lifetime task! I find that the more I can love our infinitely lovable God, our Good Shepherd who loves each of us so much more than we ever realise, the more I can trust Him! We have the gift of free will. Thankfully, our God did not create robots that would automatically love and obey Him!

I believe it is also our choice whether we accept God's forgiveness (I need this very often!) and I have discovered that there are so many times when we need to forgive ourselves! Like others I have been distressed beyond words when those I trusted were found to be untrustworthy; I have learned to forgive and found this to be liberating. However, I have also experienced rejection and deep sorrow in consequence. When I have longed for reconciliation, I have discovered that 'it takes two to tango' and that, once again, I can allow God to be in charge of each of these situations.

Obviously, since the 'end of the story' life has continued with many ups and downs but always with a consistently strong and faithful God! I have had the experience of walking through 'the valley of the shadow of death', even the death of my beloved husband, Hugh; I have had moments of fear, illness and pain; but so often I am reminded of God's faithfulness and find His comfort and strength within these valleys. I am reminded at these times of the truth of who He is, particularly when I turn to the Bible; my well-loved and well-marked Bible is a powerful resource!

I believe with joy that eternal life awaits me and that Jesus is coming again. If I am able to say with confidence that I continue to find these 'realities', then so can you – and everyone else!

So I know that in all circumstances of my life I can still trustingly say, "It's alright now – God is in charge!" and joyfully agree that...

Psalm 23
...The Lord is my Shepherd, I shall not be in want.
He makes me to lie down in green pastures,
He leads me beside quiet waters, He restores my soul.
He guides me in paths of righteousness for His Name's sake.
Even though I walk through the valley of the shadow of death,
I will fear no evil, for You are with me;
Your rod and Your staff, they comfort me.
You prepare a table before me in the presence of my enemies.
You anoint my head with oil; my cup overflows.
Surely goodness and love will follow me all the days of my life,
and I will dwell in the house of the Lord for ever.

Epilogue

An Obituary for my Father

I have a copy of the Old Ealonians Association Spring Newsletter 1988, in which there is an obituary of Father who was at the School from 1913-1915. I quote:

> Ralph Lee was a member of the first intake of boys when the School was opened in September 1913, and was placed in Form 111B. Ralph became the first captain of Perceval House; he won several Form prizes, he was a frequent contributor at the meetings of the Debating Society, he swam well, played cricket for the 2nd X1 and was the Schools best Chess player. For his age, he was a highly talented pianist with an extensive repertoire of difficult classical music, which he performed at School Concerts at which he also sang and acted.

> On leaving School, Ralph Lee went into the London and South Western Bank and in 1922 joined the Hong Kong and Shanghai Banking Corporation. He was a good correspondent and extracts from his letters, as well as articles, appeared frequently in the Acorn describing his experiences and conditions in Japan. In 1928, when on Home Leave, he was a popular member of P.D. Goodall's touring party which visited Switzerland and Bavaria.

> He returned to the Bank's branch in Kobe, Japan, where he became engaged, was married and his twin daughters were born. (Not quite correct, they were born in England!) After further Home Leave in 1934, Ralph Lee was posted to Ipoh in what was then the Federated Malay States. Before the Japanese invasion, Ralph had sent his wife and daughters to South Africa, but he became a prisoner and had a hard time in Malaya and Siam...

> Ralph Lee retired to a village near Norwich, where despite ill health in his later years, he was very happy as was so characteristic of him. He is survived by his wife, Sheila, his two daughters and four grandchildren. (He was born 7th February, 1901)

It's alright now – God is in charge!

On another page:

The death was reported ... on 27th August, 1987 of Ralph Wallace, aged 86, by his wife Sheila Lee. Ralph died after a long illness, throughout which he showed great patience and bravery.

Proceeds

The author will donate half of her royalties from sales of this book to the following ministries:

Beauty from Ashes

...where people who have suffered traumas of many kinds literally find, through the power Christian Prayer in the name of our Saviour, Jesus Christ, that their 'ashes' are turned into 'beauty' (see Isaiah 61:1-4).

Read more about this amazing ministry from their website:

www.beautyfromashes.co.uk

The Burrswood Christian Hospital

...where people of all faiths or none may receive excellent care through the team of doctors, nurses, counsellors, physiotherapists, hydrotherapy, and chaplains. This hospital has an ethos of whole-person care, and lives are often transformed by the love of Christ in action. There is a church (Christ the Healer) which holds lovely healing services, a guest house, a tea room – and the beauty of the surroundings are healing in themselves!

The contributions will go to the 'Access to Care Fund'. Read more about this unique hospital from their website:

www.burrswood.org.uk

St Alban's Church, Frant

...as a contribution towards the support of their chosen charities.

www.frantchurch.org

Similar Books by the Publisher

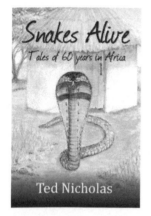

Snakes Alive
Ted Nicholas

From snakes to witch-doctors, from veld fires to terrorists: Ted Nicholas' life is filled with danger and adventure. Ted grabs life's opportunities as they arise, taking him from a simple farming life in Shropshire to a journey of great gains and great losses in fascinating agricultural projects within three continents.

Despite Ted's remarkable successes and business ventures, he acknowledges that his greatest gain was acquired in an unexpected place at an unexpected time. An American visiting a church in Africa delivers a message that changes Ted's life...

Tracing the Golden Thread
Mary Weeks Millard

An inspiring story from the frontline of practical faith in action. Mary Weeks Millard, a quiet and unassuming girl overcomes social shyness and childhood illness and a poor educational start to aspire to her heart's call to become a nurse on the mission field. She tells her own unique and inspiring life story by painting a colourful and often graphic picture of training as a nurse and midwife in the UK in the 1950s. Pressing ahead against all the odds Mary finds doors opening as she exercises her

faith in a God of possibilities These doors lead her to adventures and challenges of working in East and Central Africa in the years following independence and civil war before returning to equally challenging situations in the UK.